To us, you'll always be #1.

Thank you Rusty, for giving us so many great rides.

Rusty Wallace

RACER

Rusty Wallace
RACER

Photography by Kenny Kane
Text by Gerald Martin

AZTEX Motorsports Series™

AZTEX CORPORATION
Tucson AZ 85703-1046

5

Deluxe 0-89404-092-8
Hard Bound

Premier 0-89404-093-6
Leather Bound

Library of Congress Catalog
Card No. 94-77947

AZTEX Motorsports Series is a trademark of AZTEX
CORPORATION.

AZTEX Motorsports Series, No. One.

Printed and bound in the United States of America

AZTEX Corporation
P. O. Box 50046
Tucson, AZ
85703-1046

very once in awhile, you meet a person who leaves an indelible impression on your mind. For me that someone came in the form of a fuzzy headed kid from L.A. (lower Arnold), Missouri who had an insatiable desire to race. His name was Rusty Wallace and his game was Stock Car Racing. Any kind of Stock Car Racing.

The whole deal began in 1956, when Russ and Judy Wallace took delivery of an 8-1/2 pound bouncing baby boy who was born with a crop of red hair that would annotatively lead to his lifelong nickname, "Rusty."

Christened Russell W. Wallace, Jr., it wasn't long before Russ, his father, an accomplished racer in his own right, know where Rusty's interests lay. He wrecked his first pedal car at the age of three and burned the tires off his scooter at five. At age ten Rusty could do things with a go-cart that most people would deny possible. At the ripe old age of sixteen, Rusty Wallace won his first stock car race at Lakehill Speedway in Valley Park, Missouri… from then on it was one success after another. That success did not come without sacrifice.

Rusty wanted to race, so he put the rest of his life on hold. He didn't have many dates because they interfered with his work schedule. He had a regular job, but it was only there to provide sustenance for his race car. A regular meal was only possible when his Mom brought it out to the garage. His whole life was viewed through the windshield of a '68 Chevelle stock car, and his sole purpose in life was to make the race cars in front of him disappear.

By the time Rusty celebrated his twentieth birthday, he had won over seventy feature events on midwestern race tracks. He also won the most popular driver award at his home track Lakehill Speedway.

Rusty also realized he cared a little more for Patti Hall than he thought he did when she used to do his homework for him at Fox High School. Still, a big night for Rusty and Patti was when she spent the entire evening passing him tools in preparation for the night's event.

During this period of time, Rusty continued to pound the competition on the midwestern bullrings and his bond with a group of volunteer crew members, later to be known as "The Evil Gang," grew stronger. Aided by life long friends Charlie Chase and Don Miller, engine builder Don Kirn, and team members Paul Andrews, John Childs, Dave Wirz, Dave Munari, Jeff Thousand and others, Wallace went on a short track rampage, winning in CARA, ASA, ARTGO, USAC, WARA, ALL-PRO and a host of other associations, amassing a total of 202 victories by his twenty-third birthday.

For his birthday, he married Patti.

In 1980 Rusty experienced two of the most memorable experiences of his career—he drove in his first big-time NASCAR event, at Atlanta Motor Speedway—and Patti presented him with his first child, Greg.

Ironically, Rusty finished second in his first NASCAR event, at the wheel of a car owned by racing legend Roger Penske. Ten years later these two men would race together again, and the legend goes on.

This book is an inside look at Rusty Wallace today, the Super Star in NASCAR Winston Cup racing, with an occasional peek at the days gone by and how he got where he is today.

To me, he will always be that kid who helped me rebuild the transmission in the bathtub at the No Tell Motel, but hey, that's another story.

Don Miller

Don Miller

*D*edicated to
some of the Fallen
Heroes of Our Sport:

Davey Allison
Alan Kulwicki
Neil Bonnett

Gone…but not forgotten.

June 24, 1994

To My Fans, General Enthusiasts and Interested Readers:

I am extremely honored to have been the subject of this book.

It is a rare occasion that readers have the opportunity to have an "inside look" at the personal side of sports figures. Just like I go about my life in general trying to be the first and the best in most every aspect, I'm proud to be the first NASCAR Winston Cup driver to open up his personal life to this degree.

The past eighteen months have been full of both happiness and sorrow. The battle we had with Dale Earnhardt for the 1993 championship was a tough one. The loss of Alan Kulwicki and Davey Allison was hard on everyone involved in the sport. They were among my toughest competitors on the race track, but they were great friends of mine off the track.

The 1994 season is shaping up to be one of the most competitive years of racing and I'm delighted that my team is winning poles and races and looks again to be a factor in deciding the championship.

Several people deserve acknowledgement for their contributions to this book. Among them are Bill Brodrick for nurturing an idea, Walter Haessner for making this project happen, Kenny Kane for having the patience and drive that it took to get all the excellent photographs used in the book, and Gerald Martin for his outstanding job with the editorial contribution.

I live a pretty hectic lifestyle, but it is both pleasurable and rewarding. I think that after reading this book, you'll know a lot more about a fortunate guy who works hard at his chosen profession and genuinely enjoys relating to friends and fans. In short, you'll know more about the "real" Rusty Wallace.

I sincerely hope that you enjoy reading the book.

Respectfully yours,

Rusty Wallace

Rusty Wallace

Contents

Contents

Part One
Family & Fun

Seat of the pants driving. That's what they call it, the men and women who race cars from Saturday-night short tracks on the outskirts of St. Louis, Missouri to the high banks of Daytona, Florida and to the serpentine courses at Watkins Glen, New York and Sears Point, California. You cannot buy it, cannot lease it. You cannot steal it. Sometimes a fellow learns it and successfully imitates those who have the real thing, but only a few are blessed with it from the first time they climb upon their fathers' laps and grip the steering wheel of the family sedan.

Such a racer is Rusty Wallace. His seat-of-the-pants feel for a race car on southern Sunday afternoons is the final and most crucial link in all that has come before—from the revving engine to the drive train to the oversized tires—all delicately balanced on a fine-tuned chassis, all the products of the multimillion-dollar technology of what has become perhaps the most popular sport in the United States—NASCAR racing.

And there is a certain feeling. Rusty Wallace knows it. The one that, more than any other, separates the *best* in the business of stock car racing from those who *would be* best. It is the feeling that puckers the lower cheeks when you're riding the ragged edge at Lake Hill, Missouri or at Talladega, Alabama when you teeter without losing balance, when you grit your teeth and hardly flinch, when you get that good feeling that comes only when you've dared the devil—and won.

Judy Wallace also knows that feeling, having more than once savored it on a short-track Saturday night. Judy Wallace, Rusty's mother, was a powder puff queen back when, once in awhile, the barriers were lifted that separated the men who raced from their women who watched from the grandstands.

She raced. She won. She felt that special feeling, and she reckoned it was the right sort of stuff that her husband, Russ, had for so long felt in the seat of his britches, when he was culling the also-rans and making haste to championships on dirt and asphalt bullrings. And for the Wallace family it was not *just* a good feeling, it was to become a common bond that carried from one end to the other and all around the dining room table when supper was blessed and racing was served among other vittles that nourished the lot of them, Russ and Judy, and their boys Rusty, Mike and Kenny.

Thus it is not surprising that the question never

was asked: Would the boys go racing? There was nothing to discourage, nothing to encourage. It was a given. It was a hobby then. A hobby that consumed more of their lives than Russ's vacuum cleaner business, and for one—for Rusty—it was a launching pad to stardom, an altitude that none of the racing Wallaces at that time, in the late '60s, could imagine.

Today, they are one of stock car racing's most prominent families. While Kenny and Mike have tasted the good life and the good stuff of NASCAR racing success, Rusty, driver of the Penske South Ford Thunderbirds, has become the epitome of what Winston Cup superstardom is all about. He is a Cup champion who in 1993 was the sport's most prolific winner. Hard-nosed and aggressive when the groove was moving up and the laps were counting down, today he is idolized by tens of thousands of fans and emulated by those who would drive in his shoes.

But, there is a price to pay for such success. It is a balancing act on a high wire that spans all aspects of life—personal and professional—and the higher the stakes, the higher the wire. He has learned to perform, balance himself and juggle at great heights—without a net.

Early Days

When Rusty buckled up for the first time, back in St. Louis in the early '70s, there was no big picture, says Don Miller, Rusty's best friend, long-time counselor, agent and business partner.

"Rusty Wallace didn't want to know about anything except Pepsis, chocolate doughnuts and racing," Miller recalls. "He didn't care about anything else.

"He needed some help."

And by leash or by example, Miller helped, Rusty followed and it all came together, the racing and the business of racing. Today, he can call the shot with confidence when a million-dollar deal is going down. He can build a race car from the ground up, drive the wheels off, and win.

He has become a meticulous perfectionist who demands the same of his associates. At his shop he will roll a twisted air hose into a perfectly coiled snake. On visits to his parents' home he goes so far as to straighten dishes, align salt and pepper shakers, scour his mom's

All dressed up and everywhere to go. On this night in December of '93, the Wallaces were among the most highly honored in Winston Cup racing at the year-end awards dinner at the Waldorf-Astoria in New York.

And yes! He really does crease his own jeans with a travel iron—and spray starch.

kitchen counter. He even carries a steam iron in his luggage and personally creases his own Levi's. Expertly.

"If you had known him ten years ago and to see him now, he has really, really changed," Rusty's wife, Patti, relates. "He pays such close attention to detail. They tease him about being so meticulous, about how things have to be perfect. But he pays attention to every detail and it has paid off. He has come a long way.

"If I don't go to a race on Sunday, if I'm at home, I clean all day because when he comes walking in that door Sunday night, I want it to be perfect, so he can come in, have a nice meal, and if it's early enough, be with the kids and me. If he came in and one window was dirty and he was looking out, he would clean it. I've noticed such a difference in him since his first relationship with Roger Penske in 1980. I think he realized that first go-round how important it was as a person and in everything you do to look nice, dress nice, and I think he really got that in his head and it stuck with him."

But back in the '70s, in Rusty's early days as a late model driver in the Midwest, he was anything but polished. The hair was a mop, the sneakers untied, and the jeans were never creased. Didn't matter, he figured. Wasn't important. Only one thing counted and that was the best thing in life: whatever went fastest on four wheels.

He was determined. So broke and so determined. Judy would go the extra yard, sneaking Rusty a credit card when he needed fuel for the return trip home, just in case he didn't finish in the money. Russ the racer understood but still complained. He wondered what would become of the boy.

"He couldn't figure it out, how I kept going when I was dead broke, not a nickel and begging and borrowing," Rusty said. "He kept asking, 'How long can this continue. You can't keep doing it.'

"He wanted me to race, but he thought it would be a hobby. He had no idea it would be my profession."

Even now that Rusty has become a superstar, Russ still cannot stand it—the tension on the high banks, the occasional controversies, the bumps and bruises that come a racer's way whether or not he has the right-of-way or he did it the wrong way. And in Russ's eyes, Rusty is right. Always.

"The only problem I have with Dad is when I have bad luck, it just kills him," Rusty says. "He can't stand it, gets very, very nervous watching the race. He was a racer, a track champion. He won three track championships, in Springfield, Missouri; St. Louis; and Granite City, Illinois.

"He used to race Friday and Saturday nights there. It was the Schraders—Kenny's father—and my

Rusty pauses—once in awhile—to grab a burger and refreshment.

dad. Then he quit when Mike, Kenny and I got actively involved; wasn't enough room for all of us to do it.

"Now he goes to as many races as he can, loves it, but when I have bad luck, he goes nuts. He paces. He can't stand still. He hides his face, paces up and down pit road.

"He wants to know every little detail that goes on. Sometimes he and I get after it, because he wants to know the money in all the contracts, everything, and I'll say, 'Dad, it's none of your business.' And he'll say, 'Okay, okay, I won't pay any attention, but boy, I sure would love to know.' I love it, going back and forth with him.

"Now he's one of my biggest fans. He calls three, four times a week, wanting to know what's going on. He gets *Winston Cup Scene* and it says something in there and he'll say, 'Well, it says here that…,' and I'll say, 'Aw, they're full of crap,' and he'll say, 'Well, I didn't like what it said and I had to hear it from you.' And he's the same way with Kenny and Mike."

Russ, like Judy and like Patti, had figured Rusty, Kenny and Mike would continue racing, but the *Sport of the South,* Winston Cup racing, was a world away. Perhaps a decent future in ASA, perhaps a break-even hobby. And even when Rusty proposed, Patti figured racing would be just a part of their life after marriage, not the all-consuming life that it has become.

Family

They married in 1980, Rusty and Patti, seven years after their racing families met at Lake Hill Speedway in St. Louis. Their three children, Greg, Katie, and Stephen, like their parents, know only the racing life, though because of Rusty's success, racing is much more a centerpiece of their lives than when Russ and Judy were packing up their boys for trips to weekend shows.

Rusty was seventeen, a racer since he was sixteen. Patti was fourteen and loved the company of the new Wallace on the racing block, the one with the late model Chevy that was faster than most, the one with the thick, frizzy mop of hair. Though one day he would get down on his knees and propose to her, first he used all that charm on the girl who could get him through school while he played with his toys.

"I did all his homework for him," Patti recalls. "His life was racing, even at that point. He didn't care about school. He just wanted to graduate, get his diploma. His life started *after* school when he could go home and work on the race car.

"He had to go to summer school one year, and, bless his heart, I think the teacher just wanted to get rid of him. She told him to copy all the pages in the last chapter of the book and at least she would know he read it if he copied it. I had to copy it for him, and she passed him.

"I wasn't a big school person either but I knew how bad he wanted to get out and go on.

"His family had all the ingredients that a good family needs. They were close, good morals, not just a big academic family, and all Rusty cared about was racing. They had a little garage beside the house and he'd work on his dad's car…

"When we first started going to races, I was young, too young probably to comprehend the fan-insider difference. But once we got into it, it was something we took for granted.

"That type racing wasn't like racing here where there's a definite difference. You never thought about racing ever being on this scale."

"There's something to be said for those days 'back when,' " Rusty says, and he realizes that most when he spends some precious time with Patti and the kids.

"One day Greg was asking me some questions and I'd answer something and he'd come back and ask another, and I had something on my mind when he asked," says Rusty. "And I'm thinking, 'Why can't I get patient? Why am I doing something all the time ?'

"So we went into the bedroom, sat down on the floor and I leaned back against the bed, propped my knees up and said, 'Come here, get all your stuff and bring it in here.' What it was, he's so far ahead of his grade they want to move him up, do some special things with him, and he had picked these certain courses to take, and the bottom line was the courses were the hardest courses in school. I said, 'Why these?' And he said, 'I'm not sure I can do it, but I think I can. I know this stuff and I really think I can. And if I can, I'll be the Number One kid in school.'

"So we sat there for almost two hours, picking these courses for next year. I'd tell him what I thought and he'd agree or disagree. We went back and forth, we finally agreed on it, I patted him on the back and told him I'd see him at six in the morning."

The next morning Greg was up at six to turn on his computer and check the weather for Rusty who was preparing to leave for the airport, off again to the business of keeping a sponsor happy.

Greg turned in the courses for next year and felt good about it. "But I felt good about it, too," Rusty said. "It was just him and me and we figured the deal out. Usually, I'd have been putting a fire out at the shop, or thinking about one."

It was a rare but welcomed occasion. And it would happen more and more, Rusty promised himself. Which would draw applause from Patti. She misses the man in her life, and worries as Rusty's death-defying, barrel-rolling crashes of the past flash through her mind more than ever. She despises that part of the game, but even as she misses him, she gently encourages, occasionally even pushes, because it is not just her life, it is his passion and their life, present and future.

Wall-banging at Lake Hill and Granite City was one matter. Short-track accidents rarely took a physical, mental or emotional toll. Back then racing was just what

they did on weekends. It was expected. It was what they always had done. It was sandwiches in the grandstand, and those Pepsis and chocolate doughnuts. Even after they moved to Dixie in '83 and success on the track began to creep into their lives, Patti did not worry. He was still her high school sweetheart, hair cropped closer, driving faster cars, keeping longer hours on the road, earning more and bigger headlines, and more money.

Even the squabbles with his first car owner, Cliff Stewart, and later with Raymond Beadle, owner of the Blue Max team, were taken in stride. It was a sport steeped in controversy. The children were so young and she was so devoted. And her man was so invincible.

"When Rusty started driving," Patti recalls, "it was something you *knew* he was going to do. The fear factor at that age didn't come into it. The reality of what the outcome could be didn't hit you.

"But since then, oh yeah. Rusty had a terrible crash at Bristol [Tennessee] about five years ago and that was the first time I really thought about the reality of what could happen. We were young, building a career, a home and I was watching the kids grow and I didn't really think about: 'What if this happens?'

"The crash at Bristol kind of got put aside...then in 1993, so many things happened. Both of his crashes. There's nothing like having to watch something like that. It's terrible enough when you see it and it's another participant, like Darrell [Waltrip] at Daytona or Davey [Allison] at Pocono [Pennsylvania]. It's horrible to watch that when you know it's your husband in the car.

"You get older, grow up, and you start

thinking...he's probably going to race ten more years. That's fine. That's what we do. That's how we make a living. Then you see, for instance, Neil Bonnett [crashed and died February, 1994 at Daytona]. And I'm sure he and his wife had the same talk about how great it would be when he retired, got into something else. You think about the time when the kids will be grown and you'll have more time, more fun together."

Rusty's not ready, though, to notch the calendar, to set the day and the year he will retire from driving. He is at or near his peak, winning like never before, going like never before, and when he does slow just enough to think about tomorrow, he sometimes thinks about what they probably have missed, the 'normality' of most families' lives. But he thinks, too, about the life he wants down the road for himself and his family, about the opportunity at hand to provide for the time when he silences the engine that last time and climbs through that left-side window and walks away.

He thinks about Patti, about their kids, about those rare times when he can sit a spell with Greg and help him pick the courses. The pride abounds and this racer, almost always so intense, softens when he talks about how much they all mean to him.

"Patti," Rusty says, "knows better than anybody how to put me in my place. When the fans are out there jumping up and down, trying to act like they're idolizing you, she'll put you right back in perspective. She'll say, 'You're just ol' Rusty.'

"She's a lover, my best friend and she's a very, very quiet, to-herself person. You'll never see her out

Beautiful beast. It's Rusty's '27 Model-T Ford Coupe, powered by a 450 horsepower V-6. (left page)

Even street rods sometimes need a master's touch to stay in tune.

17

there wearing flamboyant clothes on pit road. You'll see her in a pair of jeans or a nice pair of slacks. She takes care of the kids, she's a mother and she's not into the social stuff. She hates it. Sometimes I wish she'd get more involved because sometimes you need to do that, but she doesn't like it. She would just as soon stay in the motor home and watch the race on television or go up in the grandstands and watch it.

"She's super, super good people. She's a fan and loves the sport. But she's not a *fan* fan. She's a *Rusty Wallace* fan.

"I've been trying to get her to go to more races. We have the motor coach now and I want it to have a home atmosphere, with my family in it—not lined up with people from front to back, like it's a hangout. I want to spend more time with her.

"And I'll tell you something else about Patti. She's a super good judge of character. I'll be thinking about having somebody work for me and she'll say, 'That guy is not a good guy. He'll mess you up.' I'll say, 'You're wrong; you're wrong.' But she told me that about two people, and I'll be darned if she wasn't dead on. I would disagree with her to the living end, and she'd be dead on."

Greg and Stephen are like day and night in many respects. Greg is the academician who has taken to the strategic side of the sport. Stephen, for the time being at least, is chocked full of the old man. He knows what he wants to be when he grows up—if he can get someone to help with the homework.

But it's really neither Greg nor Stephen who runs this household. Patti, of course, does her part, and Rusty, when the road isn't calling, chips in. But look no further than Katie to find the Wallace who just about every day gets the show on the road.

"I'm not saying this just because she's our daughter, but I am *so* impressed with her. She gets up at six every morning. Everybody else may be asleep, but she's up. She comes into our bedroom and tells us she's up, then she goes back to her room, dresses, makes her bed, fluffs the pillows and takes the puppies outside.

"And that's just for starters. She goes to the kitchen and makes coffee for me, then goes and gets change for Stephen's lunch and puts it in an envelope for him and then wakes him up and helps him get dressed.

"She does this all the time, just to give Patti and me maybe thirty extra minutes to sleep. We roll out of bed and there's hot coffee and the dogs are out and, the best thing of all, she's a straight-A student."

And Stephen may follow Katie's lead. But there's probably too much of the old man in this younger son.

"Stephen has a go-cart and absolutely no fear,"

Rusty explains. "He's not scared of anything. He took the go-cart and drove it head-on through the garage door, waiting for it to open.

"He gets on that go-cart and plays chicken with the garage door; he's flipped it end over end, knocked himself silly, and he just does it again.

"He's a daredevil. He got on the swing set one day and he kept going higher and higher, just to the point the chains on the swing started to give. And all of a sudden, there he was, stretched out on the ground, his legs spread, hardly breathing. He scared Patti to death. But do you think that was going to keep him off the swing set?

"Hey, he might be the happiest, most lovable, funniest kid in the world. And, believe me, he's not scared of anything.

"Greg's at the age where he's starting to go to more races and he's getting into it, especially the computer stuff. He clocks all the cars every lap—loves the races.

"He's quiet, but he's coming out of that shell and he aces everything in school, straight-A's, on the Honor Roll. He's in band. He was rated Number One in school on a big award day, a geography competition. He aced that and he's Number Seven in North Carolina in a big academic program. What is it?"

Stopping in midsentence, Rusty frets and frowns, as if his Thunderbird had been pushing a bit in a high-speed turn and for the life of him he couldn't solve the problem.

On the lake and in the wind, it's one of Rusty's few but welcomed outlets from a racing star's hectic go-go schedule.

It's time to cruise, but first a moment of contemplation. Be it boats, airplanes or race cars, Rusty makes sure his equipment is fit, fast and safe. (left page)

Part One

Cruisin', and loving it on Lake Norman.

"You know," he said, "I'm supposed to know all of this…

"But Greg is about two grade levels ahead. He's so smart it's unreal. I got him a computer and I keep adding to it and it's huge now. He has CD-ROMs, all kinds of equipment and programs. I bought a program where I could get all the weather, live radar all over the world. I get up, wake him up and say, 'Hey, Greg, how about getting the weather for me?'

"He'll have me a computer printout, all the weather for me. He'll say, 'Okay, I have live radar for you. What else do you need?' "

"That's sort of the way it is," agrees Greg. He just wishes, sometimes, that his dad could get the hang of what he's trying to teach him.

"But he hasn't caught on yet," Greg says. "No matter what I do, he just can't catch on."

It is a light moment, shared among Patti, Greg and his father in the comfy confines of the motor coach,

their hideaway within the race track walls. The coach is nestled among others whose careers—or sponsors—have afforded them such convenience. All the conveniences of home—swimming pool excepted!

Lifestyle Perspective

Describing his lifestyle, Rusty says, "It's kind of a sheltered life. I have a good time, make good money and I do my stuff. But I can't just load up the guys and go down to the local bar."

And, especially in the Carolinas near his home, he cannot, without detection, pick out those little private things that make a house a home, or bring a rousing cheer from a son or daughter, or a blushing *ooh* and *ahh* from the woman in his life. So he discovered during a trip to the mall to buy "something special" for Patti.

"I went in Victoria's Secret at ten o'clock in the morning to buy my wife a Valentine's gift…and I looked

up…a lot of people were looking through the window at me, watching me walk around. I walked out and about ten people were out there waiting for me. It's like every move you make sometimes, they're standing there looking at you, like you're a weirdo.

"You try to avoid it but you can't. So I just do my deal and put my head down and plunge through it."

And Patti grits her teeth and does the same, most of the time, sharing her man with those who worship the ground he races on. She is, by nature and upbringing, a quiet woman who still clings to memories of a lifestyle that was so much simpler, and she still is overwhelmed by the immensity of the sport and of its following.

She tries to think of Rusty, of herself and her children as normal, average people. So it is at home. But on the road it is quite a different life.

"So many fans are so good to him, so loyal, put him on a pedestal," Patti said. "And when *you* think you're just normal…I've never gotten used to that. He's

been in Winston Cup for ten years and the last five he's become very popular.

"I go shopping on a Saturday, to the hardware store, whatever, and I see all the families—the husbands, wives and the kids. They're out on their day off, having a good time being a family, being together. And that doesn't happen for us very often.

"Rusty, Thursday through Sunday, is at the race track, and Monday through Wednesday he's at the shop. It has changed a lot with him being part owner of the team. He takes that very seriously. He's at that shop with the guys and if he's not there he's at an appearance for Ford or Miller.

"I miss him. I wish we had more time to spend together, just a day and not do anything. We did that in March and I can't remember the last time within the past year.

"It's the only life the kids know, the racing life. To them, it's 'Dad's job.' They're proud he's their dad, but

Stephen, Katie and Dad at home.

A bare-headed champion, and a champion,
perhaps, to be, with helmet at the ready for
go-cart racer Stephen.

Together, again. A Wallace family portrait. Greg,
Patti and Rusty (rear), Stephen and Katie (front).
(left page)

Where there's a Wallace, there's a set of wheels close at hand—and whether it's a fine-point tip for Patti (middle photo) or looking over his shoulder at the would-be competition, Rusty is at home astride his Harley.

Easy rider—with an urge to thrill. (right page)

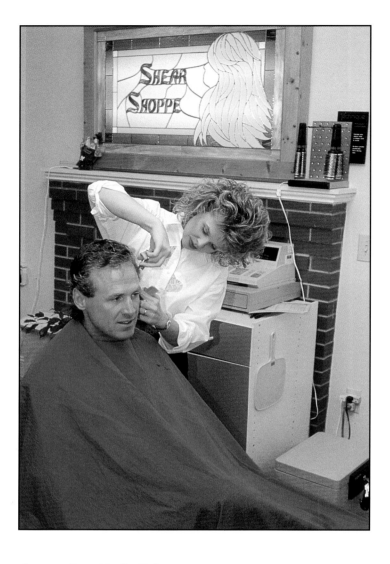

Come on, Rusty! Smile. Haircuts can be shear *delight.*

All buckled up and off to work.

they don't see the celebrity, and I think that's good."

And so does Rusty. He still remembers those Pepsi and doughnut days—sometimes even longs for them.

Things That Get Gone in a Hurry

Occasionally, he lets down his hair, pulls up a brew with the boys, or straddles his chopper or fires up his hot rod and puts 'em into the wind.

And he and Don share a love for planes that goes beyond necessity. If he had his way, Rusty would sprint between assignments in the cockpit of an F-16. He and Don check out a show now and then—contemplate, then put on the back burner, the urge to buy a vintage MiG 15 or a two-seat fighter.

His planes are his escape. Air time is a time of tranquility that he finds in so few other places. He can kick back with family and friends while his pilots pull duty, or he'll take the seat, himself, whenever there's the urge.

"Some people may say he's not book smart," Miller says, "but he got his pilot's license faster than anybody I've ever seen. He took the books and he went into a coma and studied his butt off. He reads a lot about aircraft, specifications, aero; he's really deep into high-tech aircraft.

"He does want a jet—and he'd handle it fine. I've been with a lot of pilots, from C-130s to fighters, and Rusty has two or three really good pilots. But he is one heck of a pilot. He's not a hot shot, he's not going to roll around back and see how close to the ground he can come, but he's the most scientific pilot I've ever seen and it tears him up when something happens to somebody in an airplane.

"He knows how to get the very most out of it without putting it up against the wall. He never pushes it."

Airplanes, motorcycles, vintage hot rods. Things that get gone in a hurry. And then there's the turtle's pace, the rare days at the lake, lazing on the family's house boat, taking that big deep breath and exhaling all of the unanswered questions about shocks and springs and going faster, inhaling the moment, being the dad, the husband, the friend.

"Three things I do to kick back," Rusty says, "fly my airplane, even when it's for business; that and going to concerts and playing with the boats, the Wave Runners.

"Like one day in the spring, about eighty-five degrees and beautiful. We threw a few beers in the cooler and I put Patti behind the wheel and I got up front, put those sunglasses on and about fell asleep.

"All of a sudden, 'Bam!' It was a sandbar. I thought it had torn the boat in half. But it was fine. Hey, did we ever have a good time.

"It's one of those fiberglass pontoon boats, and I put a 2.5-liter Black Max motor in that sucker, and it'll haul butt for a pontoon boat. You can ski behind it!"

Or just stretch out, tune out and turn up the volume as some of his favorite characters do their thing.

"I've always loved rock 'n' roll music," Rusty continues. "Some of my favorite bands are ZZ Top and .38 Special, sometimes a little Lynyrd Skynyrd. But if I'm a fan of any band, it's .38 Special. Those guys are good friends, they call me at home all the time, gave me one of their big albums, framed it and presented it to me at Atlanta during the 500 in March [1994].

"I get home and the phone rings and I pick it up and it's Larry, the head bass player: 'Hey, man, congratulations.'

"I like some of the country and western. Didn't used to because it was so twangy-wangy. But lately I'm starting to really like some of it, like Brooks and Dunn. But none of that old stuff.

"We went to a ZZ Top concert, parked our big Miller Genuine Draft coach in front of the coliseum and had a big hospitality thing set up and the crew guys all hung out there. It was great.

"We'll load 'em up in my King Air sometimes, take off to a concert, rent a couple of limousines and pack the crew in and go, and they treat us like a million dollars. It's a lot of fun and I like to keep my team's morale up."

But he's not the sort of person who can step away from the sport for any length of time. It is his business and his obsession. If he stopped for long, he would perish, Miller believes, because neutral is not on his gear shifter.

Not long ago, boat racer Reggie Fountain built a part-boat, part-rocket for Rusty, who wanted something that would wake the depths of Lake Norman, north of Charlotte. It was the sort of aquatic machine that, at speed, would take a fellow's mind off all except what he held in his hands: a throttle and the lives of those along for the ride of their life. It was powered by two blown big-block Chevy engines and, as Miller described it, "This thing was a personified butt-kicker."

They talked about going for it, taking it to the limit on a still, flat-water day, but there never was time.

"Then one day Rusty comes in," recalls Miller, "big smile on his face and he says, 'Come on, close your books and throw your pencils away, we're going to the lake.'"

The "home stretch." Once in a while a fellow can put his feet up—rather than down— and go places.

Rusty used to get "down and dirty," too. The subject of conversation is dirt-track racing as Rusty and a mini-sprint fan check out the hardware.

Part One

"I don't even want to think about how fast we were going. It was an off week, nobody on the lake, and we burned every ounce of fuel that thing had in it.

"We came back, talked about what we were going to do next, and we never got on that boat again. Ever. He gave it back to Reggie and Reggie built him another one, and he never got it. He went down and took pictures, talked about how beautiful it was, and never got it.

A shame. Truly a shame, Rusty says now as he recalls the stinging bite of the mist, the exhilaration of the ragged edge on the water.

"I had won the championship in '89," Rusty said, "and Reggie built me a beautiful 31-footer with twin big blocks that ran about eighty miles an hour. I took it out a few times.

"The next year he built me this boat that was so awesome—a 33-footer with 525-cubic-inch super-charged big blocks. It would run ninety miles an hour

and it looked like an ocean liner going down the road. Fly, man! And he painted it solid jet black and put a No. 2 decal up on the bow and a Mercury Marine decal. Geez. This was a pure-bred rocket. And we took it to Tampa [Florida] to use as the pace boat for the APBA offshore race.

"I'm holding the flag, we're running about seventy, cooking, and we'd peel off to the side and I'd drop the flag. Here were these 46-footers with 4,000-horse-power—*vvvvvrrrrrrooooooommmmm*.

"But after that day, we went home and I was real busy with this team, and I was trying to patch things up with the old team and here I had this beautiful, breath-taking boat. Reggie owned the boat, but he says, 'It's your boat if you'll come down here and let me give you instructions on it.' I never made it down there and one day Reggie called and said, 'Sorry, man. Somebody just has to have it. I'm going to sell the boat.'

Concentration, chrome and contentment. So it is when the rubber meets the road. (pages 28/29)

The center of attention he soon will be…but for now, a quiet moment before the New York awards banquet.

Mirror, mirror, on the wall, who's the fastest of 'em all? (left page)

"It was a bad deal. He had worked so hard, specially for me, and I screwed it up. I feel bad about it that I couldn't get down there, but I don't feel bad because I was looking after the team."

Too Big of a Hurry

Which, Miller said, is Rusty just being Rusty. But he wishes sometimes the kid would take a bit longer to enjoy a Pepsi—or a Genuine—and a doughnut.

"He doesn't have any time at all," says Miller. "He tries to spend time with Patti and the kids, and occasionally, when we go out, we have a heck of a time, but we just don't get to do those things. He has a street rod, and talks about going out and buzzing around, but it doesn't happen.

"I wish he would back off a little, but it's not hurting him yet even if he is burning the candle at both ends. And, you know, he has turned into a really good businessman because of one thing: he's always in a hurry."

"Too big of a hurry," says Kenny, Rusty's younger brother who when he was eleven years old was scared and scarred by *banzai* Rusty, the Missouri flash. Back in the late '70s and early '80s Rusty was too eager to care that his pockets were empty and his credit limit full. All he knew after the checkered flag waved was that tomorrow was coming in a hurry and there was another flag to chase. No time for pit stops.

And one night it happened. It was bound to happen, sooner or later. Judy still regrets allowing Kenny to tag along. Could have been disastrous. Instead, it was hilarious.

"They had run an ASA race at Fort Smith, Arkansas," Kenny goes on, "and we had a motor home and a race car hauler. We were in a restaurant eating

The music men: Greg on sax and Stephen (below) on a soon-to-be humming cart.

and I had to go to the bathroom and they took off and left me.

"I walked out and nobody was there. I started to walk home and home was six hours away. Little did I know if I had kept walking I would have ended up in Florida. But I finally called home, crying, scared to death, and Mom and Dad contacted the Arkansas and Missouri state patrol and the cops ran down the motor home—it was a convoy that had the lowest grade motor home you can get and a bread truck hauler.

"The state patrol stopped them and asked for Rusty Wallace and the cop asked where I was and Rusty told him I was back in the hauler. Then he went back to the hauler and asked where I was and they said I was in the motor home.

"They went back to get me and instead of Rusty feeling sorry for me, he was mad. Oh, he was mad."

"Of course I was mad," Rusty explains. "He got

Nose to nose with "man's best friend," and one of Patti's favorites, too. And is "Peaches" spoiled? Why, of course!

left because he couldn't pull the toilet paper down. It was stuck."

Rusty rolls in laughter. But Kenny still doesn't think it's funny. And to this day, Kenny always announces his intentions in a restaurant when he has to go.

Especially when Rusty is in a hurry. Which is whenever he's not asleep.

Part Two
RACING

Groups of men, some in matching team colors, some in soiled blue or white work clothes and almost all of them fidgeting with stop watches, gather just behind pit road and keep score in the final scrimmage of the week, the last chance to size up the competition.

The drone of unmuffled gut-straining V-8 engines punctures the air and reverberates off the concrete walls of "The Rock," North Carolina Motor Speedway. One car, then another and another speeds along the front straightaway, RPMs cresting before the men at the wheel rein in the horses and allow their mounts to set, settle and breathe for an instant.

Then back to the whip again, lead foot to floor pan, accelerator down—all the way.

It is Happy Hour, the last practice session before the Goodwrench 500. The sun courses westward, shadows stretch up over the retaining walls, and the stock car chauffeurs squint into the sinking sun, driving deeper and deeper into the shadowed turns that loom as black vertical walls.

And the stop watches tell their tales.

Rusty Wallace is flying. You can tell by reading the watches, by reading the smug confidence on the faces of his teammates or the disconcerting lip-biting among the clock-punching competition.

His feathers had been ruffled for the better part of the week before the Goodwrench 500, the second stop of the 1994 Winston Cup season. He usually doesn't fret about what has passed, but an unexpectedly early departure from the season-opening Daytona 500, after he had been caught up in a multicar crash, still stung. His debut in the Penske South Ford Thunderbird had been spoiled and his ego was a bit bruised, too, for he had had something to prove. He had promised in the winter offseason that he would make believers of all those who said the switch from Pontiac to Ford was folly.

And it wasn't just the marred debut that pricked his thick skin. His act was together, he and his mates were absolutely focused and dedicated. But just when it seemed the haunting memories of a tragic '93 season would abate, there was new reason for Rusty and the rest of the Cup family to ponder and to try to cope with what too often in their sport, business and life is inevitable: as surely as stock car drivers race and dare to ride the ragged edge, they sometimes will crash, occasionally they will be injured, and once in awhile someone will die.

So it had been during Daytona SpeedWeeks '94. Even before the green flag waved to send the field on its way in the Daytona 500, Neil Bonnett and Rodney Orr had died in crashes during practice. And though Rusty is not the sort of person who dwells on the dark side of the sport, neither does he take his good fortune for granted. He seems to be immune to intimidation on the track, but he readily concedes that he has been frightened in race cars and by other race drivers and by the violent crashes he has watched through his windshield or in his rear view mirror.

Dwell on it? Those who do cannot suffer what Rusty suffered in '93 and return with the foot just as heavy as always on the accelerator. Ten times in 1993 he made his final race day stop in victory lane. And almost as many times and whenever his post-race tribute was allowed by NASCAR, he had smoked the tires and revved his engine, spun his mount 180 degrees and in a wrong-way, clockwise victory lap, remembered fallen champion Alan Kulwicki. And after young Davey Allison died in July, Rusty had saluted both after each win. Though both Allison and Kulwicki died in air accidents, their loss was deeply felt by the Cup family.

Surely, he and the rest figured, '94 would be different. But no. Even before race day Sunday at Daytona, before the crash that crushed his and the team's hopes of a successful debut with Ford, the woes of the business again were manifested in the deaths of two drivers, and the Daytona disasters tugged at Rusty. Everyone had wanted so much to get on with life, to always remember the men but forget the bitterness of the '93 season.

It wasn't to be.

But now, for the moment, he is behind the wheel, lost in concentration and in his love affair with his machine. Nothing else matters. It is Saturday afternoon at "The Rock." All else except the Ford, the track, and the view have been shoved out of mind. It is time to focus. It is Happy Hour. And among the Penske South crowd, happy faces all around. Rusty is flying.

And you can tell—when he unbuckles, bounces from the cockpit and the grin spreads wide enough to dimple his jowls and wrinkle his brow—Rusty is in his element. Come tomorrow, the competition will be in trouble.

Part Two

It's what's up front that counts, and usually you can count on Rusty to be there, behind the wheel of a potent piece of Black Magic.
(page 35)

And so it was the next day. Daytona, as the shadows again crept over the walls atop the high banks of North Carolina Motor Speedway, was all but forgotten. Rusty Wallace had humbled the competition. His point and that of Penske Racing South had been proven. Ford's Dearborn crowd with the "better idea" was swaggering, the champagne was flowing and the St. Louis leadfoot who a decade earlier had moved south by southeast on a hunch and a prayer again was in his element.

Indeed, he has come a far piece.

Winston Cup

He got an opportunity to drive a Winston Cup car full time in '84, and just like that he loaded up and took off to North Carolina to drive Cliff Stewart's Gatorade car. He had won the ASA championship in '83, kicked their butts all year long, won all the big races, and in December of '83 he went to the ASA banquet, took his winnings, loaded his car and moved to North Carolina—Rusty, Patti and Greg.

"It was the big league and I couldn't see it going anywhere but up," recalls Rusty. "There was nothing to slow it down. But when I came down here and started racing 'em, it was a lot tougher than I ever thought it would be, a lot tougher, and I wasn't good at the politics part of it. I had never had to deal with that. I always called my own shots, built my own cars, made all the calls on race day from the car, when to pit and when not to pit, everything.

"The thing I couldn't get used to—couldn't

believe—was that I had had so much success and [then] I came down here and couldn't hit my butt. I wrecked everything in sight, couldn't get the car to handle. Even Darrell Waltrip, at the time, said he was surprised, that he thought I'd do a lot better because we had raced together a lot when they would come up and run in ASA.

"Actually, the 'culture shock' wasn't that bad because Darrell, Bobby Allison, Dale Earnhardt, a lot of those guys came short-track racing, to races I was at. And I was the hot dog in ASA, so they'd all come up to me asking questions. When we moved to North Carolina, I knew those guys pretty well—it wasn't like they just dropped me off in the middle of some field. Neil Bonnett, Earnhardt, Bobby Allison, Darrell—I knew 'em all. So I wasn't scared to death."

But he was intrigued—and at times infuriated—by the cantankerous Stewart, one of the sport's all-time characters, hilariously funny on the one hand, a demanding, salty-talking taskmaster on the other. A High Point, North Carolina, furniture manufacturer, the diminutive Stewart had once dabbled in NASCAR racing and had begun to dabble again when he called on Wallace. It's surprising they lasted as long as they did, the high-strung driver who had always called his own shots and the equally high-strung, strong-willed car owner, with an ever-present cigar between his grinding teeth, who made his will known to all, no matter the scene or circumstances.

Rusty's departure wasn't the smoothest when he left Stewart in '85, but he still respected the car owner who gave him the opportunity. Rusty knew he could

From bare skin…to a high-gloss finished product. Such is the transition from the ground up at Penske Racing South.

drive Cup cars, he just couldn't get Stewart's guys going as fast as *he* wanted to go.

After '84 and '85 with Stewart, Rusty changed teams. Five races into the '86 season with Raymond Beadle's Blue Max, he won at Bristol.

"Then I won again at Martinsville [Virginia] and we took off," Rusty said. "You have to earn respect—entrance—into the circle of drivers, so to speak. After the first win, maybe they said I was lucky. After the second one, they couldn't say it was luck. That was a real important win."

Although Rusty didn't win with Stewart, he learned how to play the game. Coached by old friend and advisor Don Miller, he learned to bolt from a dead horse when opportunity knocked.

"That was a love-hate relationship," Miller said of the Wallace-Stewart years. "I spent most of my time trying to settle Rusty down. I knew it wasn't going to work. It was a fiasco. I was all over the country at the time with Goodyear tires, the short-track development program, and he's down here racing and living in North Carolina. It was a long-distance relationship.

"He would call me and say, 'I've got to get out of here.' He had talked to Larry McClure and I talked to Raymond Beadle. We had been in drag racing together and I had known him from time to time. He said he would pay Rusty a percentage and I told him he couldn't do that. He had to have a salary. I made him put the money in escrow and pay him a weekly salary."

Miller shakes his head as he recalls those early volatile years, when Rusty unwittingly jumped from the frying pan into the fire—from Stewart's cars to Beadle's as the replacement for Tim Richmond. Miller figures that Stewart, in comparison to Beadle, could be a candidate for sainthood.

Rusty's guaranteed salary for the first year was just $40,000, but he was eager, hungry, and playing in a new and higher league. He wanted the Beadle ride and he took it.

"Whatever it took," Miller said of Rusty's determination to leave Stewart and his eagerness to find a winning horse. And Beadle had a good young crew who wanted to win, having had a taste of victory with Tim Richmond. Rusty would rather have driven for McClure, but he took a seat in Beadle's car. The rest is history.

That history now includes more than thirty Winston Cup victories, one Winston Cup championship and almost ten million dollars in earnings. A winner on the most elite of stock car tours, it all began for Rusty in '86, with Beadle and the Blue Max team. Even in the throes of madcap controversy, they won the sweetest of NASCAR crowns, the Winston Cup title in 1989.

It was a team that seemed to thrive on calamity, that barely made ends meet, and won even when the payroll was not met. Rusty begged the courts to void his contract with Beadle. It was a team that eventually disintegrated but refused to quit even as it fell apart.

Quite a contrast to the well-deserved but hard-earned luxury that Rusty and his teammates now enjoy with Penske South—perhaps the best of the lot in Cup racing. The volatility of the Stewart and Beadle days is gone, not that every working day is a piece of cake. The

"Talking Parrotts." Todd (left) and crew chief Buddy (center) talk a little turkey.

Aerodynamics. It's the name of the game in speedway racing. And there's no better "aero lab" than the wind tunnel, where Rusty (left) and crew prepare a new Thunderbird for a test ride.

Rusty bends Gary Nelson's ear. Nelson is NASCAR's No. 1 cop—the Winston Cup competition director whose job is to enforce the rules of competition, conduct and safety.

three partners, Wallace, Miller and Penske, are all intense, highly motivated men with hard-shelled egos—ambitious men who are accustomed to success, having learned to live with failures, persevere and go on. They are demanding of their teammates and encourage comparable enthusiasm and a healthy lust for success.

Ironically, the ambition and the competitive drive that now steer Rusty are much the same as during the Stewart and Beadle days. The difference is a much steadier hand on the wheel, a wiser and more focused athlete and businessman. It is not a craving to arrive that drives Rusty, it is a craving to continue competing and excelling at the highest level. And to understand that craving requires a look at his roots before '84, before Beadle and even before Stewart.

Beginnings…in a Barn

The roots are Russ and Judy Wallace, for sure, but the beginnings of the route to the top of the stock car racing world were seeded in an old barn behind a veterinary hospital in Ladue, Missouri.

"I used to live in Chicago," Miller said, "but…I had taken a job as the vice president of marketing for the nation's largest engine-rebuilding company. I was a drag racer and I also had a street rod. I didn't know very many people in St. Louis, so I went to this shop and Rusty was working there, doing some welding, general stuff, and we were talking about going racing and he said something about the 'famous Lake Hill Speedway.' "

One thing led to another, Miller went out to Lake Hill, met Russ, Judy, Kenny and Mike and shortly thereafter Rusty, Miller and a guy named Charlie Chase set up shop together in Ladue. It was actually an old barn behind an animal hospital, and they shared the rent.

"It was where we worked on our cars," explained Miller. "I worked on my race car—ran factory experimental, an altered wheelbase car—and I was really intent on building this street rod. Rusty would help me; I would help him."

Rusty's very first heat race was in a Wallace "family" car that Russ had given his son. He won from the start, won because his father knew the short-track game inside and out and because, like his father, Rusty had that seat-of-the-pants knack, more than enough courage to be dangerous—

though he rarely was—and forever was chasing THE dream.

Ken Schrader Remembers

"I started racing in '71," Winston Cup star Ken Schrader said, "and Rusty started in '72, at the same little race track.

"We were pretty raw, as far as everything goes, but I had won the hobby championship and wound up fourth in points and Rusty came out in '72 with a nice little Chevelle and a lot of ability and ran good right off the bat.

"He didn't start at the start of the year because he had to wait till he was sixteen. He had better stuff, but I had a year's experience on him, and we were good friends—but it got tested pretty good, too. One time we decided to see who could hit each other the most times and we both were going to get suspended but they fined us a hundred bucks, which back then was a lot. That's when he was dating my sister; I knew that wasn't a good deal, us racing and him dating my sister. But I went off and started driving midgets and he started traveling with the stock cars.

"We were too worried about how we were going to get to the race track the next weekend to worry about what was going to happen in Winston Cup. Then our deal got sidetracked there for awhile when I started racing midgets and sprints."

The Potossie Flash

But even as Rusty spun his wheels—sometimes going nowhere—he pursued his hobby and made ends meet by knocking out feature wins with regularity on tracks in Missouri, Wisconsin and Illinois.

Enter Chase, the St. Louis fireman, a big, jovial, ever-needling fellow who loved the short-track game and helped pay the rent at the shop he shared with Wallace the kid and Miller the business strategist who was determined that Rusty would make it—once he turned the corner.

"Charlie," Miller said, "is the kind of guy who'll always be irreplaceable, but he doesn't want anything to do with our big-time racing. He wants to come down, spend a little time and leave. His idea is that if he comes down occasionally, he will keep us straight so our heads will fit our hats. He's the biggest aggravating S.O.B. I ever met. If a man has a nerve in his body, he will find it. He's a phenomenal friend and he'll always be there. But if you show him one weakness, something that you're terrified he'll do to you, you can

Sometimes, it seems, telephones are part of a race driver's anatomy. There's always one more call to make—or one more call on hold.

Part Two

"We enjoyed going to the races, raising a ruckus. Everybody helped out, four or five guys who hung out at the shop. They helped get the car ready and he couldn't pay anybody. Rusty never had any money to pay a crew, so it was all volunteer help.

"I told him, 'You can keep doing that—weekend racing—and probably never go anywhere. You might have a really good time but you're going to have to get a regular job (which he had at that point, working at the vacuum cleaner shop). But to be successful at this thing, you're going to have to do it *all the time*, focus on what you're doing.'

"He was working at the vacuum cleaner shop for his father and his uncle and then coming home at night and working all night on the car with the guys. All of us had regular jobs, and we did that at night.

"We sat down one day and set some goals. You can't just go off like a shotgun and expect to be successful. So we created a company called Poor Boy Chassis, and we started making frames—chassis for race cars. We'd sell the chassis in order to fund his race car.

"There were little sponsors along the way, parts sponsors, some tire deals and things like that that made it easier to do. A guy by the name of John Childs who owned a big tire company put some money into the thing so Rusty could get a decent truck and a trailer, and we put Childs's name on the side of the car."

take it to the bank that he will do it.

"And it all started in that barn one day. Charlie had somebody else driving his car, a stock car, and Rusty was working on his stuff and I was working on a street rod. Well, there's a place called Potossie, and Charlie had a dirt car driven by a guy he called the Potossie Flash. He looks at Rusty and says, 'I'm going to fire him and put you in it, Wallace, see if you can drive it faster than your mouth works.' And that's really how it all started. Up to that point Rusty's daddy had given him a couple of cars to help him start racing. But from that point on it was *Katie bar the door*."

Time to Focus

Miller, who had joined Penske in the early '70s, continued to go to races on the weekends with Rusty, and he continued to open doors for the rambunctious young driver.

The basis of the relationship was one friend helping another. But Miller, steeped in marketing and public relations experience, prodded and primed Rusty, telling him that to succeed as a race car driver, he had to succeed all the way around or the success would not last. When you're making money, he told Rusty, you should invest it so that when the day comes when you can't drive a race car, your family will not starve.

"But, as it was," Miller said, "it was my motorsports fix on weekends. I had three kids and a house, so I guess you can say I took what I wanted to do and did it with Rusty.

One of the best ways to get a handle on the competition is a hand on the stop watch. It's a pit-wall ritual as Todd Parrott and Rusty collaborate and clock a car at speed.

A set of Bosch plugs. At the ready, these are the sparks of "life" that bring an engine from silence to the sound of thunder.

The Evil Gang

By the late '70s, Rusty was knocking 'em dead in the Midwest, winning track championships while compiling more than 150 wins in a three-state area.

While down South, Red Farmer and Bobby Allison were leading the Alabama Gang, back in and around St. Louis, Rusty and his sidekick Miller were known as the "Evil Gang," so dubbed by Allison when he used to knock heads with Wallace and Company on the Midwest short tracks. Actually, he so christened Miller, a spinoff from Evel Knievel, because Miller had so many pins and broken bones from racing accidents.

Bobby would pull his rig into one of the bullrings, catch a glimpse of Wallace and Miller and warn everybody, "Here comes the Evil Gang." And Wallace and Miller, infatuated with the new moniker bestowed by the southern stock car hero, went so far as to have a uniform patch designed, a patch they wore to short tracks all over the state of Missouri: 'The Evil Gang.'

"We were pretty wild back then," Miller reminisced. "If you could think about it, we did it—twice."

But Rusty, for the most part, still was a no-name among stock car fans outside of the Midwest. Allison and other NASCAR hotshots knew the name, of course. When they traveled to the Midwest, reaping appearance money from promoters anxious to pay the freight for a NASCAR name, more than once they were snuffed by such drivers as Wallace, Ken Schrader and Dick Trickle.

A round of wedge. A crank or two can significantly change a car's handling characteristics by shifting chassis static weight.

Tune-up tools await a quick plug check.

Rusty was notching his belt, adding to his credentials, even if his name had not become household. He won the USAC stock car rookie-of-the-year crown in '79 and the ASA national championship in '83. And when he first hit the dirt in USAC stocks, he was in yet an-other new element. Not that it slowed him.

"He went to Du Quoin, Illinois," Miller said, "and he talked to A.J. Foyt about how to run dirt. Foyt clued him in, and he has that phenomenal feel, to relate to what somebody says and actually feel it out. But he goes over there, and believe it or not, I can't remember where he qualified, somewhere in the top ten, and he won the race. Foyt finished third. Rusty was rookie of the year and finished second in points. And he built the car from scratch."

Penske Racing South

Between the USAC rookie year and the ASA championship season in '83, Rusty also honed his super-speedway skills, occasionally drifting into NASCAR country to test the Cup hotshots on their own turf. Before joining Stewart in '84, Rusty entered eight Cup events during a three-year span. No flash in the pan, he was the future of the sport—and he showed why from the very start.

In 1980, he had never seen the monstrous asphalt trioval that was cut into an Alabama valley at the edge of an ancient Indian burial ground. It was a strange—and very, very fast—place, Big Bill France's dream come true. Haunted

Part Two

by Talladega Indian spirits, some said. Whatever, it was the scene of bizarre accidents and upset victories by men who previously had never won. Miller, Rusty's friend and confidante, had lost a leg at Talladega Speedway—the Alabama International Motor Speedway—in a pit road accident. Miller's life had been saved that fateful day, in fact, by Buddy Parrott, the man who now calls the shots in the pits for Penske Racing South. But, in 1980, Miller figured the time was at hand for Rusty to try a super-duper track. Rusty, of course, couldn't wait.

"He wanted to do it," Miller said. "He had won all those track championships and he needed to pick out something where he could get some recognition.

"We were all pretty broke, but he needed some superspeedway experience and I told him the best way was to go to Talladega and run that USAC car in a Grand American race. Now here's a car that he had won a dirt track race with at Du Quoin, and he took that same car and bubbled up the fenders and everything and made a new nose for it and bolted it on to that USAC car and went to Talladega and qualified on the outside pole at 202 miles an hour and won the race.

"When he qualified, I told him to just make a complete lap and not to overextend himself. He went out and ran two laps and he came back in and said, 'Don, it's like running down a black tunnel with a wall at the end when you see the banking.' He had never seen anything like it. I looked down and his left leg was jumping like crazy. It scared the crap out of him and he wasn't ashamed to admit it.

"I asked him if he really wanted to do it and he said absolutely.

"When people tell me nowadays that you have to have ten different cars, one for every type track, I think about running on dirt one week and two months later sitting on the front row at 200 miles an hour at Talladega.

"The last lap of the race, he ran a lap at 202.2 and beat Ritchie Evans to the line."

Rusty also entered two Cup races in 1980. And in his very first Cup race, at Atlanta, in a Chevrolet Caprice that had been shoved into a corner at Penske Racing, Rusty finished second to Dale Earnhardt, the man who would become both friend and competitive nemesis, a man who, with Rusty alongside in the years to come,

The mark of a champion. When a master of the trade, such as Bobby Allison, painstakingly makes a point, listening usually is well-rewarded.

Two old hands at winning: Rusty and longtime friend and partner, Don Miller. (left page)

In the garage, a pensive Rusty mentally runs down his own pre-race checklist. (page 44)

And after the listening—and after the winning— it's time to talk to the media.

would provide Winston Cup audiences with some of the most intense, spectacular and heated duels in the sport's history.

The 1980 deal was a spur-of-the-moment business arrangement that began as idle chatter at a Christmas party. Miller tried to talk Penske into footing the bill for a Miller-Wallace effort, and after a chat with Rusty during a test session, Penske agreed to back the effort for two races. He liked Wallace's grit, his thirst for victory and, opportunity provided, Rusty proved his point. Two races for Penske in 1980 and it was over. But the seed had been planted for a partnership that in 1991 would become the foundation for what now is one of the sport's most successful teams.

"It all goes back to when Don introduced me to Rusty when they were friends and running ASA and then we made our first run at Atlanta," team co-owner Roger Penske says. "I've always watched him. I've been consumed by what we're doing but Don has always stayed close to Rusty.

"I look back over the years, and I look at the drivers we have now. Wallace has the talent like Rick Mears had when he brought us to the front in IndyCar racing, consistently, winning Indy and the championship. Rusty has the same capabilities, and he's active with the car and a motivator with the crew. When you're in this business in NASCAR and you don't have the best quarterback you can get, you're not going to win. There's just a handful of people…

"Then you have to look at his technical expertise from the standpoint of the technology between the car and the driver and the driver and the car. Then you look at how he communicates with the team. In any car racing, you're probably down more than you're up. Rusty has the capability to keep the team up. After Daytona, he said he slept for twelve hours. But I'll tell you, on the thirteenth hour he was back in that shop pumping the guys back up.

"When you've been on top, your expectations are up.

"And he is the best I've ever seen in the communications with the public and through the sponsors. We have to worry about a car manufacturer, about Miller, about Goodyear and Mobil and all these people, and Rusty always has time."

Or so it seems. Time for others. Time for business. Time for making fast cars go faster. This is Rusty's life today because such is success and its demands. But entwined in that success are those early years when the foundation was poured, before his name was a household

word. And few were those days when Rusty, Charlie Chase and Don Miller went at it less than full throttle. It always has been a rat race of sorts, a nose-to-the-grind-stone business. It's just that the stakes—and the rewards—are higher these days.

One of Rusty's most valuable assets is his knowledge of the machinery he drives. It is a knowledge that began to blossom in the days that he, Kenny and Mike, at their father's side, bent over the fenders and poked their heads beneath the hood. It is a knowledge that began flat on his back under a rolling chassis, tweaking springs and shocks and sway bars. It is a knowledge that was encouraged by Miller and honed by Penske in that two-race season of '80. It was the volatile seasons with Stewart and with Beadle and the seasons of sanity with Penske, beginning in 1991.

"The best example of the quarterback on the field, calling the plays right there on the field," is how Penske describes Rusty. "How many guys are concerned about what the tire pressure buildup is on each corner in comparison to the others after a pit stop? How many guys are worrying about how much tape is on the front of the grill? After a race today, he knows exactly what he would do differently.

"He would never be satisfied just to show up the next week with his helmet. He has to be in the shop, look under the car, be there when they start it up. He wants to know what the engine numbers are. Then he wants to be down there working at his dealership, wants to be out there signing autographs.

"The pressure on these guys is tremendous.

Ford SVO Director Dan Rivard is the man at the top and under the gun, and it's drivers such as Rusty who make Rivard's job a lot easier and oh so rewarding. (left page)

Todd knows the ups and downs—and the in's and out's of shocks, chassis setup and handling. He's a key man on the Penske South team.

Shock absorbers, coded according to "bump" and "rebound." Top teams may carry as many as fifty combinations to each track.

These big wheels, and even bigger tires, soon will be turning, taking Rusty's Ford to the ragged edge without losing grip.

Summer, fall, winter…and yes, spring. It's always the spring of the year in stock car racing, and there's a spring for every occasion.

It's one thing if you're a baseball player and you bring your hat. When you're involved in sponsors, motivating the team, the technical things he does, I think he's just tremendous."

❖❖❖❖

Penske was not gung-ho, however, when first approached by Miller about forming a new team with Wallace. Miller had been a member of the Penske family for almost twenty years and Penske was a bit beside himself when Miller broke the news that he was quitting in 1989 to launch a new team with Rusty.

"When I told Roger," Miller recalls, "he goes off in twenty directions. I love him, I appreciated everything he had done and if he ever needed anything I'd be the first guy there to help. But I told him I was going to do this with Rusty Wallace. I was going to Charlotte. I was running two companies for Roger, but I wanted to race."

The plans were laid. Buildings were started. But there still were the lingering nightmares, drawers full of court papers from the ongoing battle with Beadle. Miller Brewing Company already had said yes to a sponsorship but their hands were tied and would be until after the 1990 season.

And it seemed the more adversarial the relationship became, the harder Wallace drove. He won the championship in the middle of the battle royal with Beadle.

And Penske's appetite also had been whetted. In the beginning, the team was to be a rather low-budget, two-man operation—Rusty and Don Miller doing their thing. But Penske, still smarting from his previous foray into NASCAR battle—with only mediocre success—not only was concerned about his old friend. He also had something to prove to the good ol' boy sorts who unfairly had claimed they sent the big-time IndyCar king packing back in the late '70s.

"He didn't want to see anything bad happen to me," Don explains, "and he thought this was going to be

bad for us. And I think we were doing it because we were up against the wall.

"Then one day, out of the clear blue, I said, 'Roger, why don't you get in here with us?' He said, 'I can't do that.' But he thought it over. We were going to do it on a shoestring and we had Miller Brewing Company standing by. I had worked with Miller for eight years and they wanted Rusty Wallace.

"We were looking good and they said they'd sign up one year with Beadle if I handled the contract. I couldn't stop Beadle from getting the money but I could control it, how it was funneled through. He got a percentage, and Miller was right up front with him. They wanted to do it for Don and Rusty and didn't want anything to do with Beadle.

"It was a tough year. We were trying to do that, race and build this place. Then, about October of '90, Roger said he was going to do it, and he said if we were going to do it, we were going to do it first-class or he didn't want to have any part of it. He said, 'Tell me what you need and I'll see that you get it.' He's a good

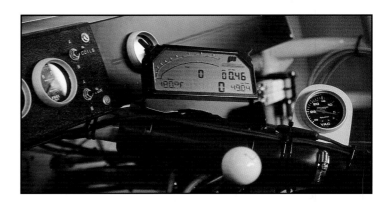

Color this 'Bird black—and gone. (pages 48-49)

This gauge, used during testing, shows the relationship between air pressure inside the air cleaner and in the air intake (cowling) at the base of the windshield.

Computer gurus Terry Satchell (l) and Nick Ollila share test data with Rusty.

"When I go into Turn One, Todd, the car lays over like this and I think we should…" (right page)

businessman. It's not like he reached in his pocket and gave us all this money and never wanted to see it again. We said, 'This is how we're going to pay it back to the company, and this is our company.'

"When we put the deal together, we had a budget of about two million dollars. Roger got involved and it doubled.

"We were going to have two little buildings. We were building cars, building engines, painting cars and doing body work. By November of '90 we had twenty-two guys in that one building. But we knew where we were going.

"In '91, we won the sixth race out. We went to the Daytona 500 and we could have won that race, and that lit a fire under these guys. That helped so much. It became a matter of, 'We've absolutely got to win a race;' that was the attitude.

"They worked day and night and it took a toll and they started falling out. People said we were fanatics. We'd be here to midnight. And so was Rusty. He worked himself into a frenzy. He was here, twisting bolts, whatever it took."

❖❖❖❖

Among the key people who now form the heart of the Penske South team are the family Parrott—Papa Buddy and his sons, Todd and Brad. And, according to

chief Buddy, the man who buckles up and puts it all on the line on Sunday afternoon also puts it on the line in the shop, and has since Day One.

"When I first started working with Rusty," Buddy said, "I put him in the same category as Darrell Waltrip, as far as feel, being smart around a race car. Dale Earnhardt has run cars all his life. I've run him on dirt and I took him to the first Winston Cup race. But he was more the kind of guy who would let you do the work and he'd do the driving. Rusty will go in there and drill a quarter panel out or re-drill it or get in there and try to weld. That's why he has so much respect around the guys.

"It's not a deal where, as it used to [be], if a driver came in and tried to work on the race car, that was taboo. With Rusty, you don't say, 'You do the driving and we'll do the work because it makes us look funny.' That's one of the things I had to learn when I came over here. You take Rusty Wallace out of the picture and he would lose that competitive edge.

"I let him get down there and wallow and get dirty and do what he wants to do, because he's having fun. That's what he likes. And he *knows* what he's doing."

"He works really close with Todd on the springs and chassis, and he wants my input as far as what the car does on the track, the feedback. He knows I'm in the

Open wide! Paul Vanderlaan and Earl Barban position a "herd of horses" for placement under the hood of Rusty's Thunderbird.

Crew chief Buddy Parrott keeps a watchful eye on Rusty at Daytona.

Yes. Even little things count. (from the left) Lee Morse, Todd Parrott, Dan Rivard and Rusty ponder how to improve the contour of an air cleaner base at a restrictor-plate race.

Rusty, in deep conversation with truck driver Earl Barban, the man who keeps the Penske rig rolling. (right page)

The Penske Racing South team, winners of the 1993 Unocal 76 Pit Crew World Championship. Standing, from left: Buddy Parrott, Nick Ollila, David Munari, Dick Paysor, Earl Barban, Scott Robinson, Todd Parrott and Rusty. Kneeling, from left: Jeff Thousand, Paul Vanderlaan, Bill Wilburn, Brad Parrott, and Rocky Owenby.

Looking pleased with their change to Ford for the 1994 season, the Penske Racing South team stands behind Thunderbird No. 009, "Midnight." From the left: Dick Paysor, Bill Wilburn, Paul Vanderlaan, Jeff Thousand, Don Miller, Buddy Parrott, Roger Penske, Walt Czarnecki, Scott Robinson, Nick Ollila, Earl Barban, Dave Munari and Todd Parrott.

game, and he'll crawl up there on the truck and say, 'Hey, what did it look like?'

"We've got a good combination going, and we want it to stay together, nobody walking out, going somewhere else, because, I tell you, a guy stays on this team and he's going to learn a lot."

And though driving a race car is—and always will be—a seat-of-the-pants art, engineering and computer technology are creating a new breed of mechanic, and a new breed of driver. As Penske said, those drivers who do not join the technology parade will be left behind. Wallace will not be one of them, although he, too, once wasn't given to graphs and graphics, of watching computer screen displays of data such as tire travel over RPMs.

"A driver can't just stand on the gas and drive over everybody," says Penske. "He has to know what makes the car better, and that's where Rusty has been outstanding.

"When they were going to start this team four or five years ago, and we decided to make the move to Ford this year, we made it as a group. It didn't come out of the clear blue sky. It was based on calculations, of where we were going.

"This business is going to get more and more technical. It's not going to be looking up at the sky and saying 'Let's put this spring in.' As we go forward, there's going to be a *reason* you put the spring in, the shock in and the way you're going to set your motors up, and if you don't understand that, you're going to get left behind.

"You can see it today. There is a handful of cars on any given day that really run competitively. That's why Richard Childress has been so successful. He has had the All-America quarterback, Earnhardt, and Childress, as a former driver, understands what it takes to motivate the driver and when you can and can't put pressure on a driver.

"A driver can't just stand on the gas and drive over everybody. He has to know what makes the car better. That's where Rusty has been outstanding."

More than a Driver— Rusty's _Totally_ Involved

Outstanding because, for a long time—even before computers were commonplace on pit road and in Winston Cup garage areas—Rusty has been *totally* involved. Take a gander sometime, at Rusty Wallace out of the cockpit. Check two or three track sites and you'll find him either atop the transporter, stop watch in hand; or squatting at the front or rear corner of his car,

Eye to eye—before going fender to fender—with fellow Winston Cup driver Dale Jarrett.

If you didn't know what it takes, this series of pictures shows the speed, cooperation and coordination needed to send your driver off to victory—and to win a UNOCAL 76 Pit Crew Championship as well. (pages 58 & 59)

NASCAR free-floating axle awaits completion of a gear-ratio change.

contemplating a spring change, talking shocks with Todd Parrott, tire pressure with Brad; or at a garage work bench, discussing an engine combination with David Evans or a computer readout with Terry Satchell or Nick Ollila.

Rusty thought computers were a nuisance for awhile. He actually rebelled against computers. It wasn't that he didn't realize the value. They were just nuisances.

"We were screwing with computers, a wire over there in the car, when the bottom line was we'd just put in the car what we wanted in it anyway," he said. "But that was naive. Looking back at it, I'm glad we rode the wave out because I'm over the nuisance part now and I've

learned how to decipher all the good information.

"Now, I get right into it. I don't know how to operate it, but I know how to turn it on. I go out, make a run, come back in and say, 'What does the computer say? Show me.' They show me and I'll say, 'Yeah, I could feel that,' or, maybe again, I didn't feel it.

"One thing it helps us do, especially with our new Ford Thunderbird...I was hearing all this detonating and we were burning pistons. It enabled us to figure out our fuel distribution really good. We could measure all of the exhaust gas temperatures per cylinder, and it really helped a whole lot.

"The car was running real good at Daytona, in

the draft, the motor I ran almost 800 miles on in testing and qualifying, he took it apart and said it looked brand new, like it had hardly ever been run. Not a scratch anywhere, fuel distribution was good. And the computer had measured the exhaust temperatures, the cowl pressure, the amount of air going into the carburetor. It took a lot of time for me to be able to decipher the data."

Computer technology and applying that technology each year become more and more integral to success. Teams are limited by NASCAR to seven test sessions a year, and a driver, no matter how good he is or how telling that feel in the seat of the pants, can deliver only so much data to his chief and other engineers.

Today, computer gurus such as Satchell and Ollila can gain feedback quickly, from everything from shock sensors to ride-height sensors on the car, aero probes, cowl pressure, even throttle response for the engine guys. The team, not just a driver or a tire specialist, learns a ton every time a driver makes a 10-lap run. As Buddy Parrott explains, "A 10-lap run today is like a 100-lap run a few years ago."

"In 1992," Parrott recalls, "we were instrumenting the cars, and I think it was a deal where we were just going through the paces. In 1993 we started with the help of Terry Satchel. He had been working with computers with a lot of different teams, and he was able to put it in

layman terms so Rusty and I could understand it. And it made it interesting. If something's not interesting, you just say, 'Aw, I don't understand that.' But just to show you how much Rusty is into computers and technology, his Christmas present to us to put on the truck this year was a shock dyno. We're one of three or so teams that has a shock dyno on our truck. He understands the value of that.

"If we had told him we wanted a shock dyno in 1992, he would have rolled his eyes and said, 'Sure, that's exactly what we need!' "

And there's yet another technical phase of the overall game in which Rusty has engulfed himself, the sometimes hair-pulling business of wind-tunnel testing where even the slightest bend of a piece of sheet metal, the slightest alteration of a fender can translate into a significant difference in a car's performance at speed on a superspeedway. A business just for those who build the bullets? Perhaps in some camps, but not for the man who points the bullets that carry the Penske Racing South logos. It is not just enough to know that it works. Rusty believes a fellow who makes a living by the seat of his pants on a high-banked Sunday afternoon also should know why it works, and aerodynamic massaging is no exception.

So when the big blades begin to whir in Ford's tunnel at Marietta, Georgia, the St. Louis kid tries to be on hand.

"I watch every move that goes on," Rusty says. "And I try to add any assistance I can. I want to know every change that's made and I want to know it well enough so somebody doesn't have to tell me."

Rusty first went to tunnel tests with Barry Dodson, his crew chief during the Blue Max-Beadle days, "and he's a really good guy in the wind tunnel, smart, knows aerodynamics, and he taught me a lot about aero," says Rusty. "I started understanding what to look for and I started teaching myself.

"The GM and Ford tunnels are completely different. It seems the tunnel at Marietta runs the air speeds faster and you get a better, truer reading about the performance of the car. All the wind tunnel numbers were different [Ford vs. GM]. When I had my Pontiac in the wind tunnel, I got the numbers and I can compare my Pontiac to the Ford. I wanted better numbers with our Fords, and I was happy with what I saw."

Still, there is no substitute for perseverance, and for trying new methods that are as much the product of a brainstorm—or even an accident—as is a computer-generated "can't-miss" suspension geometry. Such was the car that carried Rusty to most of his 1993 victories and his first '94 win. The chassis, which now holds a

more potent Ford engine and is sheathed in Thunderbird clothing, was, in some ways, a product of trial-and-error engineering. And Rusty did not take a back seat to those whose job it is to put all the pieces together before the sheet metal, the paint and the decals are applied.

"I took that car, I jigged it, and I know every spot in that car and I'm making all my cars identical to it," Rusty said. "If I wiped that sucker out, I could put it right back together. And I've never, ever been able to do that. I've always raced a car, and then I'd say, 'Aw, it's been a good one' if I tore the crap out of it, and then I'd say, 'I think this was here, think this was here.'

"But after Atlanta in '93, we took a two-inch steel plate, put the chassis on there and copied everything on it, put everything in the same exact spots, and it stuck like glue.

"And some of it came out of our butts. Some of it was by accident. But we still kept changing. We never said this is perfect. We kept trying, trying, trying."

Nuts and bolts. Sheet metal and shocks. Flow benches and dynamometers. Fabricators and engine builders. Transmission specialists and cylinder head specialists. Computer gurus and chassis whizzes. Demanding car owners, dedicated crew chiefs, and determined, seat-of-the-pants race drivers. It takes a heap of equipment, tons of money and even more talent to put it all together and, on race day, to pull it off, the ultimate trick of the trade which is to finish the day in victory lane, just a short piece down the asphalt-paved banks where the shadows stretch up and over the retaining walls.

Rusty and fellow IROC driver Scott Sharp discuss drafting technique just before the race.

Race driver and friend Mark Martin and Rusty have a racer-to-racer talk. (page 62)

Lull before the storm. Rusty moments before another dash for cash in the International Race of Champions. (left page)

If it's okay with Roger Penske, it's okay with Rusty.

65

They are the Heroes

And for those who have been a party to the accomplishment, there is no greater satisfaction, no sweeter taste in the moment of exultation, than when the spray of fine champagne mingles with the sweat of the brow and courses down dirty cheeks. So it is for the man who climbs from the cockpit, and for all who have labored through those days and nights to produce that sweetest of moments. They are men and women who often give far more than they take, but rarely is there one among them who would swap for anything those short, sweet moments in the shadows on Sunday afternoon.

They are the heroes of stock car racing, and just as they labored to get this team off the ground, they still go the extra yard, says Rusty, "because, to a man, they have more pride than any group I've ever been around, even when they're worked their butts off all day and it seems like everything is in order.

"Roger is like that. Everybody on this team is like that.

"I remember after the Busch Clash was over in February, they had an hour practice scheduled after it for Winston Cup. I'm thinking, 'We'll cover the car up.

We're set and we'll run Daytona 500 practice tomorrow.' Roger comes in and says, 'Heck, No! We've got an hour of practice. Let's use it.'

"The whole team jumped on it. He made 'em do it. We were ready to go home. He said, 'Get the car ready.' Now, we've got shocks right, springs right and we've worked like blazes, and when he said we were going to do it, the whole team is like, 'Oh, shoot.'

"We went out, came back in and made a couple of spring changes and he's out there, putting a stop watch on me, every corner, every lap, talking to me, watching everything, the whole deal.

"Then, after we got through, everybody's saying, 'Man, I'm glad we did that.' It was great. The car really hauled butt.

"Know what Roger said? 'If you have the practice, use it up.'

"He's really getting excited about this NASCAR thing, a lot more excited than I thought he would. He's really into it. It's the excitement. It's the business. It's both. And when he hires somebody, no matter what he hires 'em for, he expects excellence and he expects hard work. He wants you to work your butt off and he wants to win."

A bug in his ear? Well, sort of. Rusty hooks up an earpiece from the two-way radio used to communicate with his pit crew during the race. (left page)

From dusk till dawn, and sometimes into the wee hours; a racer's work is never done, and neither is the work of his teammates.

A measure of power, the tachometer gauges engine revolutions per minute—and 9,000 is a bunch.

And so does Rusty Wallace, whose long-laboring crew helped him uncork the champagne at Rockingham for the first time in '94, again beating ol' buddy Earnhardt to the line as he did in '93.

And in the end, at Rockingham, it was, of course, Wallace who was snuggled by the babes in victory lane. It was Rusty who was framed in the camera lens and hustled from every angle by TV sportscasters and newspaper reporters. Such is the nature of this team sport. Many labor but most often it is the quarterback who basks, just as it is the QB who, on the other hand, so often shoulders the blame when the game does not end for his bunch with a victory lane portrait.

A Perfect Understanding

At Rockingham in '94 it was a Penske family portrait again. And it was, again, Rusty taking the measure of the man he so admires on the one hand and would always rather beat than any other. Of all the men who take it to the limit, Wallace and Earnhardt form perhaps the most unique mutual admiration society in all of

Part Two

sports. They profess friendship and a friendship it is, sometimes strained, sometimes complex, sometimes as simple as a smile, a handshake, an arm around the shoulder and a joke before the dash. Through the seasons, each has tormented the other's soul. Twice they have dueled to the last laps of the last race of the season for the Winston Cup crown. Once it was won by Wallace, once by Earnhardt. Their fenders have met on occasion, and their crews in past years have been at each others' throats in exhibitions of post-race fury that followed late-race run-ins between their beloved drivers.

Parrott, perhaps, said it best:

"Yep, that's Rusty's buddy, and he'd rather race him than eat when he's hungry."

Parrott describes Earnhardt as a "rubber," a driver who rarely thinks twice about leaving a bit of his paint on another fellow's car when the laps are few and the track is narrow. He doesn't fault Earnhardt, but he said he believes there's another way to do business and that the man in his corner, Rusty Wallace, seldom creates work for the men in his body shop.

"It feels good, as a crew chief, to have the team that Earnhardt has to worry about beating every Sunday, and everybody on our team feels that way," Parrott said. "I hope we stay side by side all season.

"Rusty is a clean driver. Maybe I didn't work with him during the days when he bumped somebody, but when you can run Martinsville and North Wilkesboro [North Carolina] and Bristol, Tennessee, with the *same car* and not have to put a side on it, then that guy knows how to race a man and not rub on him.

"On the other hand, in that other corner, I don't think *he* knows how to race *without* rubbing on you. That's the difference in the two. Rusty's ready for the rub when he has to get the rub."

And more than once these two have rubbed each other wrong. But more than any other incident or accident, the frightening, barrel-rolling crash at Talladega in '93, after Rusty's car was nudged by Earnhardt's, is most remembered—and despised —by both. Earnhardt was visibly shaken and emotionally drained as he climbed from his car after the last-lap wreck and rushed to Wallace's side. He called Wallace's hospital bedside numerous times. And in the aftermath, though his wrist was broken and his championship chances for the moment were as crushed as his car, Rusty tried to heal what could have been a grudge-laden rift.

"He's a good friend, a nice fellow, and he'd probably do anything I asked him to do for me," Rusty said of Earnhardt. "But he has pissed me off a lot on the race track, some of the stuff he has done. Talladega was a bad deal. I was mad but I wasn't going to start anything because I really didn't understand what had gone on. So I didn't say anything.

"He called, he apologized, took all the blame, said he couldn't believe it happened, didn't know how he let it happen, that he was a lot better driver than to let that happen, and he didn't know why he did it.

"At the same time, I remember seeing him coming and I pulled down in front of him and blocked him off. I was thinking, 'Man, I hope he gets slowed down in time and doesn't hit me.' And then he hit me.

"So, I took part of the blame about blocking him. It's not a situation where you start pointing fingers. Yeah, a lot of people said, 'You were too nice.' But pointing fingers doesn't gain anything. I learned in this sport a long time ago that getting on the radio, hollering and screaming doesn't do anything.

"So we talked about it. Yeah, I pulled down in front of him. He was going to give me one of those nice little you-S.O.B.-you-beat-me-again-today love taps in the back, but he hit me while I was turned and got me sideways. He didn't mean to turn me over, just give me a love tap.

"But because of an incident like that, and some of the stuff that happened a few years ago, we have a heck

Sunrise at the track finds Rusty's crew still hard at work making sure all is just right with the "Genuine Draft" No. 2. Preparation is all-important for a successful drive to win. (pages 68-69)

Torque wrenches, screwdrivers, gloves and tape are among the tools of the trade for a Winston Cup mechanic.

Contemplation.

Rusty's new-found love for drag racing is shared with the legendary Don Prudhomme.

of a respect for each other. Earnhardt never, ever, ever runs down and beats on me. He doesn't do that, and I don't beat on him. We have a perfect understanding that if we start beating on each other, I'll beat on him back until it's done."

❖❖❖❖

That understanding, in Rusty's mind, was achieved in the early weeks of the 1990 season after he had won the '89 Cup title by twelve points over Earnhardt. In the second race of the '90 campaign, at Richmond, Virginia, Earnhardt rammed Wallace's car on a restart and Wallace momentarily lost control. They had dueled door to door several times during the race and Rusty led the most laps, but Mark Martin won, edging Earnhardt's scarred Chevy.

Wallace bit his lip until Earnhardt pricked his emotions the next week at Rockingham.

"I didn't say a word at Richmond," Rusty said. "The next week we got to Rockingham and he said, 'Come on man, what's wrong?' I said, 'I have something to tell you: If you ever touch me again, I'll send your butt

over the wall. I don't give a #!?*!* who you are.' He said, 'Now, we don't need to be talking like that because I can do that, too.' I said, 'That's right, and I'll beat on you and I'll beat on you and I'll beat on you. Don't touch my car ever again. You can play with all your buddies all you want, but don't pull that crap on me.' Since then, we haven't had a problem.

"Then, when the Talladega thing happened, it was kind of another thing. I watch him get out there and beat on some guys, and I don't say anything about it as long as he doesn't beat on me. And we get along real good. I have the same respect for him.

"If I beat on him, you can bet I'll get hit back. I'm talking about hitting you in the butt and spinning you out. Rubbing fenders is one thing, and he has made me so mad sometimes that I want to wreck him. But if I ever wrecked him and hurt the guy, I couldn't live with myself.

"People say, 'heck, he wrecked you and hurt you'. That doesn't count. If I got to a big track and got mad at the guy and wrecked him going into turn three and he got sideways and hit the wall on the driver's side and it

Foot to the floor and flying low—this is what they mean when they say, "AT SPEED."

Power to spare, and the 'Bird handles like a dream. But it's never, never a sure thing, this fickle game that is stock car racing.

killed the guy, I could never deal with something like that. So it's hard to retaliate on the race track and it's something I'm not going to do.

"I'd rather beat the best guy out there and he's the best out there. I love it, because he's a go-getter."

The "Man in Black" Comments

And it is a mutual feeling, said Earnhardt who in 1994 won the Cup title, holding off Rusty's furious late-season charge after he recovered from the Talladega crash.

"I think Rusty and I make each other more competitive," said the man in black. "You know when you're racing him, he's giving his all, and you're racing somebody that's determined to race you. We bring out the best in each other.

"When you're racing him you're racing somebody that's just as determined to beat you as you are determined to beat him. He's racing you to race, not in visions like some other people race you. I race 'em as I see 'em, as they come. I pay attention to all of 'em and I don't take for granted who it is or what it is. I race 'em all and I never drop my guard.

"I'm focused on everybody. If somebody's on

the inside of me, whatever, I don't drop my guard or change my style. I keep my defenses up. But it's more enjoyable to race somebody like Rusty who you know is as determined as you are."

Rusty is not one to boast about his talents, though he is supremely confident, sometimes to the point that others misinterpret, reading cockiness into comments he makes about his team's readiness or his Thunderbird's performance—which at times has been only a bit shy of awesome.

As Kyle Petty Sees It

"He has put together a good, good group of guys who like him and really believe in him," Kyle Petty says. "And they just go out and win races.

"He's not that much better than other drivers. It's the combination. It's part Rusty and part the team. You could get some other drivers and put them in Rusty's car and it wouldn't work. It just wouldn't work like it does with them.

"But going back and going over the wins last year, I give Rusty credit, because he's a great race car driver. And he's great in a lot of different ways. He knows a lot about a car, a lot about a chassis and the shocks and stuff.

"He's about thirty-seven, and if you go back and look at Dale Earnhardt or Richard Petty or Darrell Waltrip or Cale Yarborough, from about thirty-four to forty, those were their hot years and Rusty's right in the center of his hot years. He knows what he's looking for in a car. He knows what he wants it to feel like, and he can get it because he's smart enough. Put him in Dale's car, he'd do the same thing. Put him in Mark Martin's car or

Pre-race invocation on Pit Road. A time for reflection, and remembrance. From the left: team members Bill Wilburn, Jamie Freeze, Billy Woodruff, David Evans, Dick Paysor, Greg Wallace, Bob Webb, Dale Walls, Nick Ollila, Scott Robinson, and Paul Vanderlaan.

Almost ready. Car No. 2 is rolled onto Pit Road by Brad Parrott (left), Tom Polansky, Scott Robinson, Paul Vanderlaan, and Todd Parrott. Earl Barban (far right) pulls a parts wagon.

A pensive moment, reflecting on race strategy before the start of the event.
(right page)

my car and he'd probably be doing the same thing.

"Take him on back and put him in some other cars back there and he'd just be another race car driver, but that's because he's not just a great race driver, his team is very, very good, too. And I think that's what a lot of people overlook sometimes, with deals like his or Earnhardt's. Earnhardt's an incredible driver, but he has an incredible team.

"And what makes a good team as much as anything is, like Earnhardt's, you never hear any of his guys say anything about Earnhardt, that they don't like him or don't like what he does on the race track. They back him up 100 percent. If he goes out there and runs dead-on into ninety percent of the field, they're going to be standing right behind him. When the fight starts, they're going to be standing right behind him.

"And that's the way Rusty's crowd is. When the fight starts, his guys are going to be standing there right with him and they'll go toe-to-toe with anybody."

When to Gamble, When to Rumble, When to Back Off

Those occasions, though, when push has come to shove, have been few and far between. A skirmish here, a hard word or harder look there among crewmen as competitive as their driver is not unprecedented. Rusty's guys do stand by their man. But the scraps have been few because, on the track—though the scraps have been many—they have not been the sort in which fingers can be pointed at Rusty for taking a cheap shot or leaving his bumper wrapped around another driver's neck.

He takes great pride in the fact that he rarely abuses his equipment, especially on short tracks where most, at best, come away with tire doughnuts on the quarterpanels, and at the worst, with fenders and hoods missing. To win or to contend, to go doorpost to doorpost with the competition and then load an undamaged car on the truck and head home, not only is the mark of an experienced, lucky, savvy driver with smarts aplenty who knows when to gamble, when to rumble, when to back off and when to press the issue. An undented car after the battle also means less repair work for the body men, and more time that can be devoted to improving equipment and performance.

"I don't run Martinsville," explains Rusty, "and at the end all the fenders and brake duct hoses are knocked off. I take my car to Martinsville and take it back and do a few things, wash it, re-decal a couple of things. But I don't tear my stuff up. Earnhardt scrapes his stuff up all the time but he doesn't knock the quarterpanels off. He

*Out front and feelin' good—Rusty leads; Ken
Schrader in No. 25 gives chase.*

Jubilation on Pit Road. The team celebrates their first 1994 win when Rusty takes the checkered flag at the Goodwrench 500, Rockingham. Bill Wilburn (left) watches and Paul Vanderlaan (right) cheers, as Brad Parrott tosses a celebratory bucket of water to the wind.

door-marks everything up. But everybody has a different driving style.

"Tony Glover, Sterling Marlin's crew chief, came over at Daytona ['94] and said his car owner, Larry McClure, was asking him how we won all those races in '93 and ran so strong without tearing anything up. Tony said he asked Larry, 'Are you paying attention? Do you ever see that car wreck, with a scratch on it? Do you see him sliding sideways every lap?' Tony told him, 'He runs when he has to, and he's always working on the chassis.'

"I told Tony, 'You're a smart kid. That's why you do so good. You're watching.' "

When he's running side by side with Dale, Kyle or Ernie, bumper to bumper in a pack of cars and the guy ahead is holding him up, Rusty deliberates in a second or less and decides the proper course of action. There may be a hornet's nest behind him and he thinks, "Do I take my time getting around this car and take a chance on getting nailed in the rear, or do I take it into the corner and say, 'I'm tired of this; let's go for it.'

"Sometimes, when they're packed up behind you,

it's time to go," Rusty says. "If it's late in the race, it's almost always time to go."

Options, Risks, Moves, and Rewards

Indeed, it is very much the thinking man's game. The options, the moves, the risks, the rewards, are countless during the course of a race. Decisions that could make or break a driver, his car, his hopes, are pondered and executed on every lap. What's the water temperature? Lap times? The deficit? What's the margin between first and second? How well is the machine handling in the corners? Is he saving the tires? Is the line he's running consistent?

"I'll pick out certain spots around the track," Rusty said, "and I'll try to hit those certain spots every time. If there's an old beer can laying at a certain spot in the infield, I'll aim for it every time. I'll aim for a particular mark or a sign painted on the wall when I start to drift out. I try to run every lap consistently."

As Brad continues his liquid celebration, Bill scrambles out of the way while Paul and Todd raise their arms in a half-hearted attempt to avoid a dousing.

But stuff happens. No driver is perfect. No driver can do it all, miss every tire-cutting scrap of debris on the track or drive through every pileup without scraping a wall or another car. Quick reflexes are not just an asset. Quick reflexes are life savers and race winners. And no driver would start a race without some comfort that luck rides with him.

Rusty, of course, has crumpled more than a few fenders during his Winston Cup career, and no one would deny that he has a flair for the spectacular. Not that he tries, and not that he hasn't been nudged and helped along the way, but he has bent a few so badly that the carcasses had to be tossed into the junk pile. He is a master of the high-flying act, working without a net, riding out end-over-enders and barrel rolls everywhere from Bristol to Daytona and Talladega. Rarely, though, has he been injured, and most of the injuries have been minor. Remarkably, like the rodeo bull rider, he always has bounced back—quickly—and usually with a vengeance.

"I don't think about dying in a race car," Rusty said. "Honestly, I don't. I completely separate that. I can talk about it, easy. But I really feel my race car is one of the safest around, the way we do the roll cages, the way we do the seat belts, the seat installation. I feel good about it.

"The only things that scare me are fire and a sudden, high-speed, frontal impact with the wall. There's a lot a driver can withstand, cornering crashes, hitting the wall, but when you're at high, high speed and you hit at a weird angle, head-on into the wall, I think about that. If that situation is going to happen, work at trying to get the car to crash in the corner instead of head-on. There's only so much a body can stand. When Neil took that hit… Well, I've never been in that situation yet.

"We try to make the cars as safe as possible and then, what happens, happens. I can't sit there and be concerned about it. Some drivers are really concerned about it. There's a big, big name out there who is scared to death. It wouldn't be fair to say who he is, but he feels better at the short tracks, the Martinsvilles and Wilkesboros. He's petrified at Daytona and Talladega,

With ecstatic smiles and big bear hugs, Paul (left) and Brad continue their dance of joy. Though every victory is sweet, the first win of the season carries a special satisfaction.

and his wife is scared to death, too. We've talked about it.

"I don't think about getting hurt, either. I feel like I can get hurt, but when I'm on the track I don't make any weird moves unless it's the right kind of crazy move. I don't go *banzai* and say I can't get hurt. I respect the car, certain race tracks. But I'm not just sitting there, pushing the button, like a machine taking off.

"Sometimes I think I'm too timid, too safe. But just about the time I'm taking it nice and easy, some sucker beats me."

Rusty Speaks His Mind

At Daytona, when double tragedy struck the Winston Cup ranks as veteran Neil Bonnett and rookie Rodney Orr perished in crashes during practice, Wallace, like other veterans, was shaken and obviously concerned. And the more he thought about the crashes, the more he thought about other frightening incidents on the big track. The more he thought about the growing number of inexperienced Cup drivers, the more he felt a gnawing

urge to speak his mind. And he did, twice, during SpeedWeeks '94.

Few knew, though, that Patti Wallace was the person most responsible for Rusty rising to address the other drivers. Rusty's crashes at Daytona and Talladega in '93 had torn at Patti for months, and she had agreed with Rusty that some drivers, especially the younger breed, were too rambunctious, at times reckless. And though Rusty's message was directed toward all Cup drivers, he had hoped to jar the youngsters who were so anxious to make a name for themselves.

"Some of 'em were fast, too," Rusty said. "They just do dumb stuff.

"There's a way to win these races. You have to be aggressive at the right time. You have to run hard but you can't *banzai* it for 500 miles. You run when you have to run, do what you need to do but *do it at the right time.* There's a big difference in having a whole pile of balls and understanding how to win.

"And at Daytona in February, there was so much bad happening on the track, so much of that 'I'm

Astride his fabulous black 'Bird, Rusty pulls into victory lane.

Ahh! The spoils of victory—as Rusty collects a smooch from Patti and Unocal 76 RaceStopper Lisa Shrowder.

Flanked by the Unocal 76 RaceStopper (left) and Miss Winston, Rusty celebrates with a traditional champagne dousing aimed towards the media.

just going to mash the gas and see what happens' mentality, no respect for other people or what could happen. No respect for the crew members, how hard they have to work. And nobody was willing to step up and say anything.

"The problem with all the wrecks is the drivers, not the cars. They bitch about restrictor plates causing wrecks. The restrictor plate is not what runs one car into another one. And I started thinking, 'This is bull. Everybody has all these opinions about what's going on and they're full of crap. We're the ones causing the problems. And I'd had it.

"I said exactly what my heart was telling me, exactly what I thought was right. I talked to NASCAR, to Gary Nelson and Les Richter and Bill France in the office that morning about what I wanted to say. I said, 'Will you listen to me.' And they said if I wanted to say something, okay. I said it and I think about seventy percent of the people really loved it and I think thirty percent still just didn't get it. Mostly the young guys, saying we were just trying to scare them. They were saying they were going to mash it.

"Well, after all that, I fell out of the 500, got in a wreck after another guy hit another guy and I got involved. I *watched* that race. But I'd wanted to say something for a long time. It didn't take much, but what shoved me over the edge was Patti. She got real scared when we went to Daytona. She was *nervous*. Neil Bonnett got killed. Rodney Orr got killed and she freaked out. The phone started ringing at the motor home. 'Is everything okay?' She couldn't wait to get out of there. She was shaking all week. She was the one who pushed me over the

edge to make the speech. She had no idea I was going to do it.

"Then I wrecked and she came down to the hospital, looked at me and said, 'Let's get out of here.' I had never seen her move so fast. She was slinging clothes in the bags, and we hauled out to the airport. She said she couldn't wait to get out of the place. She said drivers didn't respect each other and they were going to kill somebody again.

"She had started getting that way—about half way—at Daytona ['93]. It was the first time she had sat in the grandstand and watched me wreck. She watched that thing go end over end over end and she couldn't believe it.

"Then she watched it again, on TV, at Talladega, and then, Neil and Rodney. We had just finished putting our wills together, updating—every iota of my estate handled—in case the worst happened. I felt like I was financially secure. Then, as soon as that's done, we go to Daytona and two drivers get killed and it scares her to death."

Patti's Perspective

She had always thought her man was invincible. But after the two barrel-rolling crashes in '93, though Rusty recovered quickly from his injuries, Patti began to think more and more about the dangers of the sport. She began to think about the time apart, time that both had sacrificed in order to build for their future and the future of their children.

"I was watching Talladega ['93] at home with the kids and I said, 'It has to be a Daytona replay. It's got

And to the victor…Rusty shows off his trophy after winning the 1994 Goodwrench 500 at "The Rock."

Everyone gets in the picture after a hard-won victory. (pages 84-85)

to be.' It was horrible. The kids were all screaming, upset, and you're thinking, 'Oh, gosh, I've got to stay off the phone, they'll call right away.' And that five or ten minutes it takes for them to call is like hours.

"You try to put it out of mind, the danger, thinking about the worst, but you never can 100 percent. I always thought I coped really well. I stay busy and he's always busy and our schedules are opposite. I'll be doing something with the kids and he'll be doing something with racing, so we don't dwell on it. And racing people are such a happy-go-lucky bunch. They go from race to race and when one week's over, they forget about it and go on to the next.

"But 1993, with everything that happened, it really bothered me. I realized a lot more the consequences and the reality of it.

"I've never asked him to quit. But I'm looking forward to the day he retires and goes into something else. We've been doing this our whole married life and I can see him in another capacity, maybe as a car owner or

doing something with television. I think he would be very good at that."

Racing is _more_ than Winning

But not yet, not quite yet and probably not for some time to come. He still is possessed by the fever, the urge to thrill, the feeling in the seat of his pants that courses through his body, mind and soul and, payday or not, brings to the St. Louis Kid the ultimate pleasure, the feeling that comes when you meet the competition on an even playing field and take the measure of the lot of them.

For Rusty Wallace, it is, as it was back in those barn-burning days of the '70s, the satisfaction of toeing the ragged edge and riding it without tumbling off the hurting side. It is winning, but it is more.

It is the love of the game, the love of a lifestyle, and the continuing challenge of what has become a dream come true.

Part Three
Business

The trophy has been stashed and soon the checks, the spoils of victory, will be deposited. Bills will be paid. Fenders will be repainted, the engine will be rebuilt and a few days later they will do it all over again, perhaps with the same Ford Thunderbird, perhaps with a new edition.

Race—win, place or show—pack up, take care of business away from the madding crowd, then do it again, and again.

But, there is more. Much more. There is the *business* of racing—of winning, achieving, influencing, catering, grinning and bearing—that occurs not at the track or in the confines of the spit-polished complex that is Penske Racing South, but in that big, wide world outside.

There are deals to be cut, or mulled and rejected, sponsors to be served and potential sponsors to be courted. There are appearances for fee and appearances by contract. There are charity functions and there are obligations to be honored just because a fellow owes a friend one.

There's always another obligation, another duty that calls away from the race track, away from the racing shop when your name is Rusty Wallace and you have become all you ever hoped to become—a household word not just in the Southeast, but from coast to coast and wherever the language of stock car racing is spoken.

A weekly routine? Some things never change. There's always more to do and never enough time to accomplish every task on the list. Shop talk is more than idle chit-chat. It is planned. It is serious. It is in-depth. And the first priority is whatever those glistening black Fords need to get the job done on the next go-round.

But even a fellow who thrives on going sometimes needs to back off the throttle, and on Sunday evenings, after the victory has been bagged or the wounds have been licked at trackside, Rusty or one of his pilots puts his King Air in the wind and heads for home.

"Sunday night after a race I get home and the first thing I do is turn the answering machine off. It seems everybody wants to call and bug you on Sunday night. But I have to have a little peace. I've got a favorite chair in the living room and I just want to get in there and relax in that baby, maybe watch the weather channel and see what the weather's going to be the next couple of days.

"I'll take a shower, really get to feeling good, get a little something to eat and get down there and play with the kids a little and talk to Patti. And I don't want to be interrupted by the outside world."

It's not easy, though, to sneak home when the day ended in victory lane. The messages—before the answering machine is silenced—have piled up from well-wishers with good intentions. And, on those winning Sundays, there are more than a few wheeler-dealer types who beg for Rusty's services on the following day—everything from morning talk-show hosts to souvenir vendors with a new can't-miss gadget.

But Sunday night—win or lose—usually belongs to Rusty, Patti, Greg, Katie and Stephen.

"And I've been working hard at trying to spend Mondays at home," says Rusty. "Patti and I usually try to do something together on Mondays, go to the lake, ride the boat or go do a little shopping. Lately, with the good weather, I've been playing around a lot on the boat.

"I'm gone so much, we just try to keep to ourselves. No phone calls, no nothing. No pager. There's nothing that important that I need to know about. I have a cellular phone in the car and Angela, my secretary, usually knows where I am and she'll call if there's something really wrong. But generally, don't call me on Sunday night or Monday."

Come Tuesday, though, it's back to business, and almost every week the Tuesday routine is filled with shop talk, of breakdowns—if any—that occurred in the previous race, of plans for the next event.

"On Tuesday," Rusty explains, "I like to walk around and see how everything's going, make sure the cars look like what I think they should look like. Any controversial stuff, employee problems, I'll defuse it and put the fire out. I'll look at everything, how everything went last race. And on Wednesday, it's more of the same. Then, Todd Parrott and I sit down and we start discussing the setups for the cars we'll take to the next race.

"Wednesday, things are really starting to happen. I try to get over to the car dealerships in Tennessee on Wednesday. You're always planning, more and more. And my pilot, Bill, and I talk just about every day, and we go over the aviation stuff, organizing what we're going to do,

86

Part Three

Surrounded by signs of speed—from the posters on the wall to the radio-controlled Piper Super-Cub suspended from the ceiling—ever-busy Rusty catches up on reading and phone calls. (page 87)

Nigel Mansell, PPG IndyCar and Formula I driving champion, and Rusty compare notes on the very different types of cars they drive.

Crew chief Buddy Parrott, Rusty, Walter Czarnecki, Executive Vice President of Penske Corporation, and Roger Penske caught in a jovial moment.

where we're going. Sometimes we fly two, three times a week, sometimes just once."

The average corporate pilot spends about 320 hours a year in the air. Rusty and his pilots flew more than 450 hours in 1993, and in 1990, after winning the championship, the total was more than 650.

Come Thursday, Rusty usually is back at the shop to care for final details before heading for the next track.

"I like to be there on Thursday for the final chassis set-up," he continues, "then we're back on the plane and on the way to a race track. But there's never enough time. As the season goes on it seems you leave for the track later and later. We never leave when we say we're going to leave."

And rarely is it as simple as fly in, catch a bite and hit the sack. The night before first-round qualifying often includes some sort of hand-pumping, autograph-signing social function. And such nightly functions, which are part of the job and the celebrity, often strip away "free time" after the track closes.

Rusty, and other drivers, are finding some escape in their motor coaches—luxurious homes on wheels—that are parked in secured lots adjacent to garage areas. It's not just the comforts, though; it's not just privacy. It's part of the time-saving package. A driver can grab a few extra minutes, perhaps even an hour, of rest when he can jump in the shower and dash out the door and in a matter of a few minutes be in the cockpit.

Part Three

In the cockpit, enjoying the opportunity to pilot his King Air 200. In the air or on the ground, Rusty's at home with speed. (right page)

Climbing aboard his King Air 200 for yet another flight, Rusty's always on the move.

And Rusty, whenever possible, uses his coach as his home-away-from-home. Fridays, Saturdays and Sundays are track days, almost from sunup 'till sundown, and if he's not behind the wheel or huddling with his mates, he usually is taking care of business or gulping down a hot midday meal in the confines of his coach.

A fellow must be careful not to cut himself too thin, of course, and Rusty probably never will take on much outside of racing. Some other drivers tinker with real estate, farming, all sorts of Madison Avenue-fueled businesses. But for the time being, Rusty is content to race and, well, maybe sell a car or two here and there.

"The only businesses I'm in right now are the racing business and the car dealership business. I have a percentage of a Pontiac store in Morristown, Tennessee, and a percentage of a Toyota store.

"Ray Huffaker, my partner in both stores, called me about five years ago. I was driving Pontiacs and he said, 'Hey, how about coming up for an autograph session?' I went and a whole pile of people showed up, I mean a ton. I had won the race at Bristol and it's only forty miles from Bristol, maybe less.

"So after that, he had me come in the following year, and there were even more people. Ray asked if I'd be interested in the Pontiac store. He was looking

*A relaxed Rusty looks forward to piloting his 1975
Beachcraft King Air 200.*

*While Rusty is being interviewed by phone, Roger Penske listens,
ready to add his insight and perspective if needed.*

for a partner and he's always had great success with
partnerships.

"We struck a deal and ever since, business has
increased, over thirty percent after they put the name
over the door. It's been super successful and he's been
really good to me. And then I had the opportunity to
get involved in the Toyota store and business went up
over there.

"That's all I'm willing to do right now, all I feel
financially comfortable messing with.

"I'll go there twice, sometimes more a month. I
shake hands and call on some customers, visit plants
around the area to let people know I'm interested in
what's going on there.

"It has always been super on customer service,
all kinds of awards. That dealership is one of the master
dealers for like eight or nine years in a row. It's been
No. 2 and 3 the whole time in the Atlanta zone, and
that's good.

"The thing I can't sacrifice is going out there and
having bad service and somebody call the dealership a
pile of crap. So the service has to be super good and
that's one thing I make sure happens."

Fans

Though stock car drivers beg for privacy at
times, they know that, for the most part, fans are the
people who butter their bread. Passionate in their love
of the racing game, its participants, its equipment, its
sponsors, Rusty believes they are not just to be tolerated,
but applauded and catered to. Bad apples excepted.

When he first came forth from Missouri, barely
exposed to the media, rarely abused by fans, he at first
had difficulty dealing with the new world of Winston
Cup, the prying reporters as well as fans so persistent in
their affection that they rubbed him wrong.

He was aggressive, pretty wide open with his
comments, and he saw that the fans weren't buying his
candid, ear-biting comments. The media thrived on it.
Reporters hustled to his steaming car in the garage
whenever things broke loose on the track and he was
forced to the sidelines. The reporters loved it because
Rusty would speak his mind. But the fans, especially
those aligned with the camps of veteran heroes, hated it.

"Then," Rusty said, "I decided, 'Wait, do the
best for both. Say the right things, do the interviews,

Rusty announces the Penske Racing South change
to Ford for the 1994 season.

Dan Rivard, director of Special Vehicle
Operations (SVO) for Ford, and Rusty at
the press announcement meeting.

An impromptu business meeting on a busy New York street. Rusty makes a point as Don Miller and Wally McCarty, Miller Brewing sports marketing representative, listen intently.

Dr. Jerry Punch of ESPN interviews Rusty.

*Kathryn Penske and Rusty share a light moment
over dinner.*

give the press guys what they want to hear—accurate information—but take a lot of the boasting and cockiness out of it, which I didn't mean to be doing. It was just the way I talked.'

"But I still screwed up sometimes, so I decided I wouldn't comment much on anything as far as racing goes. I just started paying a lot of attention to the car, pushing my people real hard to get them moving."

And as he pushed, he succeeded. And his legions grew. He learned to love it. Rusty signed autographs following victories until the fading day turned to night. He posed for snapshots with them and held their babies, and he became one of the sport's most gracious winners.

"In '89," crew chief Buddy Parrott says, "I remember Rusty talking about how abrupt he had been with fans, saying exactly what he felt. He said, 'You know, I was a little brash and sometimes it came out negative. Once you say something, you can't retract it.'

"I knew exactly what he was talking about. A lot of times when I've been in the heat of the battle, I've done that. But you learn to engage your brain before you engage your mouth, and that's more true now than ever

because of sponsorships and other obligations. Sometimes you can't really say what you feel, what you think. And the most important thing is that it all affects how the fans accept you. And Rusty wants to be accepted by his fans—all race fans—and I think he's getting more and more acceptance since the booing days after the incident at Charlotte with Darrell Waltrip."

There were more than a few bad apples that May day in 1989, and most of them felt Rusty was bad to the bone and as wrong as sin. He had just completed his most successful season, winning six Winston Cup races with the volatile Raymond Beadle team. His popularity had soared, but on that day, it all but crumbled at his feet after he tapped Darrell Waltrip's rear bumper, sent his car spinning and Waltrip into a tirade, asserting that Wallace had "stolen" the Winston.

Waltrip, the infamous "Jaws" of Winston Cup racing, suddenly had become the prince, and the St. Louis kid who won the Winston had become a greedy mercenary, a dirty driver. Despite Rusty's pleas that he had not intended to spin Waltrip, his meteoric rise to superstardom had been sent spiraling downward.

Part Three

*Reba McEntire, country music superstar,
and Rusty enjoy a chat.*

*Time out for a few words with Ki Cuyler,
patron of the Driver of the Year award.*

Rusty, about to be chauffeured on another round of media conferences. For a change of pace, someone else gets to do the driving.

And, as he says, there are some bad apples, even some scary moments with fans. Such, he believes, is the nature of the sport.

"It is easier for me because I don't tolerate a lot of the unfair stuff," Rusty says. "It's not easy at all for Patti. She takes every little word to heart, and she doesn't like it."

But she didn't stop that day to take anything to heart. Her hands were full of her kids' clutching fingers and her ears rang with Rusty's firm order.

"He said, 'Get the kids in the car and get out of here,'" Patti remembers. "So I did. I went home and I kept waiting for him to come home, waiting for him. Then he walks in and he has these two big body-guards with him, and I look down and they've got guns inside their little jackets. And I said, 'Oh my God, what happened?'

"So these two guys come in and spend the night in our living room. I fixed them Sloppy Joes. I hadn't planned on company."

It took awhile for Rusty to rebuild his stronghold of fans, and to come to terms with the boos that haunted him every time he was introduced. But he went the extra mile, with *his* fans—and the *opposition's* fans—because he realized what had been lost was more than fans, it was a measure of respect.

Still, there is an occasional bad apple. You can push the envelope of cordiality till it is punctured and, sometimes, you just cannot make a friend of a fellow who doesn't like Fords, or folks from Missouri, or a cool Miller Genuine Draft, God forbid.

"Away from the track, nutty fans scare me," Rusty said. "They're pulling for somebody else and they hate you so bad, go to such lengths as following you home, threatening you. It happens!

"I was sitting in an autograph session two years ago at Atlanta, and this real old redneck-looking, dirty-looking dude walks up and stops right in front of me, looks at me and he says, 'Rusty Wallace, I'm so-and-so. I'd just like to tell you I hope you #!*#*!! drop dead.'"

In wrapping up this discussion on "the other

Part Three

Part Three

In the trailer, Rusty-the-man watches Rusty-the-driver, catching up on the day's events as the media saw them. (pages 100-101)

Fans crowd around, seeking Rusty's autograph. (right page)

1994 Winston Preview at Winston-Salem Coliseum, a charitable event for Brenners Children's Hospital. As Rusty visits with a couple of young fans, Dave Marcis (center, with hat) autographs a few for the adult contingent.

Time out for autographs for these smiling waitresses.

A few young fans gather 'round to get an autograph from their hero, Rusty. (right page)

guys" fans, Rusty comments, "And there are a lot of crazy women, too."

When it comes to Rusty Wallace fans, he has a deep appreciation of them. "I want fans to be able to come to the races, enjoy them and have a good time," Rusty says.

But there are some times he needs a little privacy, a chance to wind down after practice, take things a little slower. "When I walk into the hotel, I'd rather not find fans peeking around the corners to see what room I'm in," he explains.

"I try to sign the autographs, talk with people awhile, and most understand. But, there are a few who want *more* than your time and you have to balance all that out," Rusty goes on. Like when he's trying to get something to eat, he doesn't expect fifty people to line up there for autographs.

Behind the Scene

Don Miller, the man perhaps most responsible for coordinating Rusty's go-go lifestyle away from the shop and track, has represented Rusty or been at his side for every deal that was made on behalf of the superstar, from an arrangement with a St. Louis tire distributor to

the team's current multimillion-dollar package with Miller Brewing Company.

The marketing of Rusty Wallace has been one of Miller's primary objectives for more than a decade, and his vision in the infant years of Rusty's career has yielded a bountiful return.

"The business end never stops," said Miller, who from scratch built a company for Penske—Motorsports International—that annually does millions of dollars in business in souvenir merchandise. "When automobile races were first getting some television attention, I told Rusty that it was going to catch on and be like baseball and football and basketball and hockey. That was about 1980, and I told him the guys in the driver seats, paying attention from the beginning and doing their homework with souvenirs and the collectibles industries, were going to make it big.

"When I first told him he would make more money off of his endorsements than he would driving a race car, he said, 'Ah, you're full of crap, Don.'

"But we have worked hard on it for ten years, registered his name and registered the graphic for his name and spent time building an identity program for him. And that part of the business has grown at a rate in the last seven years that it has about doubled, and now it

just about doubles every year. It has virtually exploded the last couple of years. Luckily, we were on top of our game when it was time to react to the opportunity.

"And it's all based on performance. Does he win races? All the pieces have to come together, and all the pieces have come together. But years ago when I told Rusty that we we're going to work on his name, license his name some day and develop a program for identity purposes, he didn't really take me seriously. He just looked at me and said, 'Good, I could be like an A.J. Foyt!' "

Indeed, at the time Miller first suggested his plan for the future to Wallace, the kid all but brushed it off. His deal was racing, turning left. Maybe a Pepsi and a doughnut along the way. Maybe a T-shirt with his name on it. Maybe a press kit.

"Don's always watching everything I do, like a second father," Rusty said. "He's a partner and he's my best friend, and one of the first times we were trying to get a sponsor, Don said we had to put a press kit together to let people know what was going on, who I was. We made up a thing, a piece of folding *papier-mache* stuff, printed real weird-looking. But he helped me get some sponsors and along the way we wrote a lot of themes and ballads."

Rusty still doesn't relish the paper-sorting game, file cabinets or boardroom meetings. He trusts most of the contracts game to Miller and Penske and is quick to point out that he graduated from high school with no "trick stuff," just a basic education, one year of junior college to learn a bit about engineering, and no honors.

"This is Rusty Wallace and Don Miller," Miller said as he settled into his desk chair and played both his and Rusty's roles:

"Rusty, what did you do with that stuff I put on your desk?"
"Oh, I read it."
"Did you *really* read it?"
"Yeah, I read it."
"So where is it now?"
"Well, you know, it's in the waste basket."

"I'm talking about copies of contracts, key messages. But I know what he's thinking: 'Why do I need to save it, you save it all. When I need it, I'll get your copy.' "

Miller shrugs his shoulders and chuckles again. He is most familiar with Rusty's tactics in the off-track pursuit of some business matters. He also is quite aware that there is a method in the madness. Rusty knows

Miller is taking care of business and, by relying extensively on Miller, Rusty is afforded more flexibility and more time to take care of other off-track business.

Back when they used to cut their own deals, Wallace and Miller winged it, sometimes forgoing the paperwork, rarely consulting a lawyer. They couldn't afford one. Today, not only do lawyers scrutinize voluminous contracts, so does the eagle eye of eagle eyes—Roger Penske. He signs the contracts, and as Miller said, "He's a one heck of a negotiator."

And despite his disdain for bargaining tables and paperwork, so is Rusty.

"I don't have to go and make a deal anymore for Rusty Wallace," Miller said. "He's a no-bull guy and he has the ability to cut through the crap and go for the jugular. He can get done in three hours what would take a normal guy ten hours."

Through the years in Winston Cup, Rusty's primary sponsorships have run the gamut, from such as Ramada Inns and Kangaroo Shoes to AluGuard, Zerex, Kodiak, General Motors, Ford, Bosch, Mobil and Miller.

Today, each of Rusty's personal service contracts specifies a number of days that he will be doing business on behalf of a sponsor. These average about sixty days a

year, in addition to gratis appearances he'll make related to various racing events.

Among those gratis events are several especially meaningful to Rusty, his team and his family. Whenever the Rusty Wallace Fan Club gathers, it's an affair steeped somewhat in hero worship because almost all who attend are Wallace fans to the core. It's enough to pull on a fellow's heartstrings, enough to give him pause as he recalls from whence he came not all that long ago.

Just ask Judy Wallace, who, as president of her son's fan club, knows better than anyone else where he came from. From forty members in '86, Rusty's club, although rarely advertised, now numbers more than 5,000 who for a membership fee of twelve dollars receive everything from a membership certificate to discount souvenir coupons, patches, lapel buttons, hat pins and a newsletter. The fan mail is piled into tubs at the post office and Judy, for one, tries to read every letter, whether scribbled in crayon or the polished product of a laser printer. Many of the letters, she said, are passed on to Rusty.

"The letters," Judy says, "run the gamut, from children who say, 'I'm Rusty's biggest fan,' to couples who

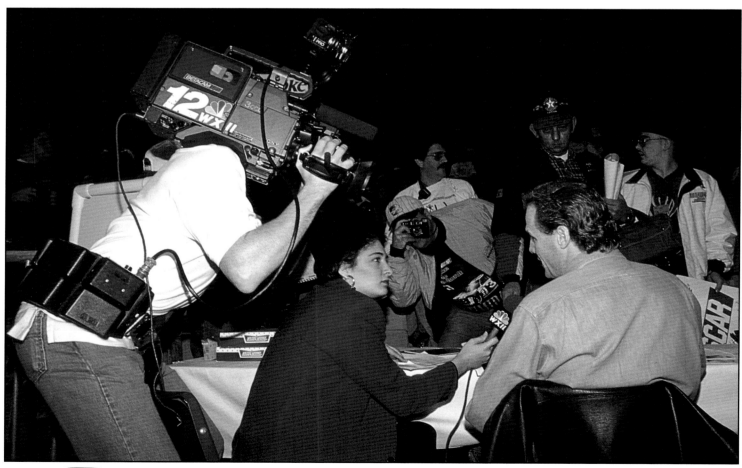

want him to be the Best Man at a wedding. Another invited him for a helicopter ride in Hawaii.

"And there are some that just break your heart, from children who are sick or from people writing on behalf of very, very sick people. When someone writes and says a child is dying of cancer, it really does break your heart, and Rusty makes a lot of personal calls to people with special needs."

Always in demand. Always on the run.

The Pepsi and chocolate doughnut days are long gone, not that Rusty is the *caviar* and *chardonnay* sort. But the St. Louis Kid has traveled a far piece down the business road since he hand-painted a sponsor's logo on that old sportsman Chevelle.

Today, the deals are megabucks, but the demands on his time and person are not without toll, be it time away from home and family or time away from the comforts of life that he has amassed but seldom can enjoy.

"We talk about the demands a lot," Patti Wallace said. "You reach a point where you're saying, 'When are you going to be home? You never spend time with me.' And then you reach a point where it's like, 'This isn't

cutting it. I'm not happy and I'm not making you happy. This is the way it is, so knuckle down and get a grip on it and let's make this deal work.'

"The way we both look at it now is that those demands won't always be there and you have to look out for yourself and your family when the time comes that you're not able to race or you don't want to race anymore."

Miller and Wallace, along with Roger Penske, are partners in the team that won ten Winston Cup races in 1993 and, after switching during the offseason from Pontiacs to Fords, became one of 1994's most formidable teams. It is a hard-nosed threesome when the chips are down on the race track, but no less hard-nosed when the chips are down in the boardroom. That's one big reason why each has been a winner on and off the track.

Much ado was made over the team's switch to Ford for '94, and hard-nosed negotiating on several occasions sent the General Motors (GM) troops ballistic. Penske called the shots and bargained with GM for a deal comparable to what the team had had for three

An extra measure of dexterity is needed here, as Rusty autographs this poster being held up for him.

Rusty being interviewed during "Stocks for Tots" children's' benefit, one of his many charitable functions. (left page)

Part Three

"Right here, please, Rusty," this young fan seems to be saying as she points to just the right place for Rusty to autograph her shirt.

(right page, top to bottom)
Somebody tickled Rusty's funny bone, as he laughingly grabs a sandwich and a "cold one." That's Jimmy Spencer in the background.

Rusty joins the Cub Scouts.

"Hobby racing." Rusty and Bill Wilburn at a sprint car race with Bill's car. Bill changes tires on the Penske crew and works in the chassis shop.

Catching up on his reading at 25,000 feet, in his King Air 200. (pages 108-109)

Autograph hunters way-lay Rusty backstage at the NASCAR Awards Banquet.

seasons, not more, as some in the GM camp charged. And after waiting for two months for GM to match the previous package, Penske turned to Ford and put his cards on the table.

"All we wanted was the same deal we had had for three years," Penske said. "We had won fourteen races, more than any other GM team during that three-year period. But for some reason they decided they didn't want us. And when you're not wanted, what do you do? You go down the road."

And do what even a lot of experts said couldn't be done. Two races into the '94 campaign, Wallace again was in victory lane. And the Daytona debut was going quite well until Rusty was caught up in a crash not of his own doing. Penske, the risk-taker, rued the crash but couldn't wait to get on down the road to Rockingham. Rusty had his best run ever going at Daytona and David Evans and the engine room, in their initial effort, had turned out a potent engine for the 500.

The victory at Rockingham confirmed what Wallace, Penske and Parrott had believed, what they had told the second-guessers, including several big-name GM drivers who had predicted the team would not win until sometime deep into the '94 season—and the victory at Martinsville reconfirmed the Penske South team's confidence in the switch to Ford.

There were moments, of course, when Rusty looked back over his shoulder at the team's '93 track record, the double-digit list of wins, the near-miss in the driving championship chase, and pondered the switch. But he had learned long ago that even when Penske's trail sometimes led a bit off the beaten path, it usually led to success.

"He's one of the most successful businessmen I know," Rusty said. "And it's funny; he'll comment on something that seems really far out, and he starts hammering on you and hammering on you to do it. And then, when you do it and you get deeper into what it is he wants you to do, it becomes less and less ridiculous and you start feeling stupid about yourself because you didn't listen to him at the very first.

"He's really made suggestions to me that sounded off the wall, but they work. I used to strive to find things to disagree with him on. I used to disagree with him a lot. But he has proved me wrong so *many* times that I find myself listening to him more.

"He's a perfectionist. He demands perfection and I love it. I like to have real neat organized things. Performance, the same way. He never leaves anything carried over or out of control. His Indy Cars are always perfect. He's a workaholic."

Takes one to know one, of course, and Penske

says he sometimes is amazed by Wallace's untiring efforts away from the track. Rusty, he says, is the best driver in the business and that he would lead any stock car team to the front—off and on the track.

"He doesn't get the credit he's due," Penske said. "He's outstanding in all aspects, technically, as a good driver, and he motivates the team and he's fantastic with the sponsors. I think it's his enthusiasm. In this business you've got to be enthusiastic, whether you're a car owner or a crew chief.

"He anticipates on the race track, but he also anticipates from the standpoint of what the sponsors want. I've had sponsors come up to me and talk about how good he has been, even when we were down, whether he was talking to Miller distributors or Mobil people or the car dealerships he represents."

"It's part of the job, that's all," Rusty says. The appearances, the autograph sessions, the motivational speeches. And most of it comes easy—much easier, in fact, than the on-track bit. As publicist Tom Roberts remarks, "Give him an idea of what you want, and he'll pull it off. He can do a lot of homework in a hurry when he has a speaking engagement, and he can go in, pick up on a few key items and really knock 'em dead. He's a natural when it comes to speaking, and he genuinely enjoys it."

But he also can be the taskmaster. He expects a pursuit of perfection among his troops in the shop and his crew in the pits. But he expects no less of himself and, as when he labored alongside his mates when the team's racing facility was under construction, he believes in setting the example and pulling at least his share of the load.

As Miller says, it may be a game, but it's more. It may be sport, but it's more. It's work, a job, a never-ending quest that can—and does—pay big bucks. But it also exacts a heavy price

"You know," Miller said, "he'll come in sometimes when he has a free minute or two and he'll sit down and say, 'Don, I remember when you told me I had to clean up my act, when you told me if I was going to wear Levis, I had to iron 'em. And I'd think you were crazy.'

"Well, to this day he still puts the creases in his Levis. Tell him once, and if he thinks it's a good idea, he jumps on it with both feet.

"One thing I've learned over the years is if you're going to have a team, a high-profile team, no matter what you're doing, you don't go out and do it with a bunch of bozos. This is like war. I tell 'em all the time that this is our war and that we're going to go out and bomb the competition.

Trying on a new role, Grand Marshal Rusty drops the green flag for a
celebrity race at Port Royal Speedway.

Rusty and Hall of Fame driver Cale Yarborough
share a private joke prior to the celebrity race at
Port Royal Speedway, Pennsylvania. (left page)

Winner Jimmy Spencer (left) and Grand Marshal
Rusty wave to the crowds from victory lane as
unidentified flagman holds the checkered flag at
the end of a celebrity race at Port Royal.

Rusty kibitzing with Jimmy Spencer before a
celebrity race.

Rusty takes time to pose for photos at a children's hospital benefit in Winston-Salem, North Carolina.

Behind the scenes details include picking out fabric and clothing designs for Rusty Wallace paraphernalia. Interior designer Pat LaGere (right) also worked on Rusty's house.

Seems like Rusty can't walk into his office, but that phone's got him again. Busy, always busy.

"We're going to take our best fighter plane and our best pilot and our best bombs, and we're going to have the best wings and the best canopy and we're going to go out and knock them out, because if we don't, they're going to comeback and get us. That's the only way to approach this."

Because it's not just a sport, it's a business. And it's a business the fighter pilot, too, believes in. That's why he jumps on it with both feet.

Both feet on the accelerator.

Part Four

RUSTY WALLACE CAREER RECORDS
(1980 through 1993 seasons)

SUPERSPEEDWAY

Year	Races	Won	2nd	3rd	4th	5th	6th-10th	11th-31st	DNF	Poles	Outside Poles	Money Won
1980	2	0	1	0	0	0	0	1	0	0	0	$22,760
1981	4	0	0	0	0	0	1	0	3	0	0	12,895
1982	3	0	0	0	0	0	0	0	3	0	0	7,655
1984	20	0	0	0	1	0	1	10	8	0	0	127,880
1985	20	0	0	0	0	1	5	4	10	0	0	164,965
1986	21	0	0	0	1	0	10	7	3	0	0	264,440
1987	21	2	1	1	1	1	5	5	5	1	1	413,185
1988	21	5	5	3	0	2	2	3	1	1	3	792,700
1989	21	3	4	0	1	1	4	5	3	3	1	630,925
1990	21	1	0	2	1	2	3	5	7	0	1	272,730
1992	21	0	0	1	0	0	5	11	4	1	0	368,940
1993	22	5	1	2	1	2	2	4	5	2	0	757,335
Total	218	18	13	11	6	10	42	59	59	10	6	$4,468,049

ALL RACES

Year	Races	Won	2nd	3rd	4th	5th	6th-10th	11th-31st	DNF	Poles	Outside Poles	Money Won
1980	2	0	1	0	0	0	0	1	0	0	0	$22,760
1981	4	0	0	0	0	0	1	0	3	0	0	12,895
1982	3	0	0	0	0	0	0	0	3	0	0	7,655
1984	30	0	0	0	1	1	2	17	9	0	0	195,927
1985	28	0	0	0	0	2	6	8	12	0	0	233,670
1986	29	2	0	0	2	0	12	9	4	0	0	557,354
1987	29	2	3	2	1	1	7	6	7	1	2	690,652
1988	29	6	5	4	2	2	4	4	2	2	4	1,411,567
1989	29	6	4	0	2	1	7	5	4	4	2	2,247,950
1990	29	2	3	2	0	2	7	5	8	2	1	954,129
1991	29	2	0	3	2	2	5	5	10	2	2	502,073
1992	29	1	2	1	1	0	7	12	5	1	1	657,925
1993	30	10	4	2	1	2	2	4	5	3	1	1,702,154
Total	300	31	22	14	12	13	60	76	72	15	13	$9,197,811

Career Record in Chronological Order
1980

Date	Track/Event	St	Fn	Laps	Money	Status
3/16	Atlanta/Atlanta 500	7	2	328/328	$14,250	Running
10/5	Charlotte/National 500	25	14	325/334	8,510	Running

Penske Chevrolet #16 at Atlanta
Norton/CAM 2/Gould/Penske Chevrolet #16 at Charlotte

1981

Date	Track/Event	St	Fn	Laps	Money	Status
5/24	Charlotte/World 600	P21	30	204/400	$2,020	Accident
8/2	Talladega/Talladega 500	P19	21	147/188	2,225	Engine
10/11	Charlotte/National 500	B19	6	331/334	6,750	Running
11/18	Atlanta/*Atlanta Journal* 500	B31	29	156/328	1,900	Oil Pres.

P=Pontiac B=Buick—Drove Levi Garrett/Benfield Racing Pontiac #98 at Charlotte and Talladega; drove Child's Tire #72 Buick at Charlotte; drove KangaROOS Buick #72 at Atlanta.

1982

Date	Track/Event	St	Fn	Laps	Money	Status
2/14	Daytona/Daytona 500	B19	37	40/200	$4,500	Engine
3/21	Atlanta/Coca-Cola 500	B23	35	71/287	1,355	Engine
5/30	Charlotte/World 600	B23	29	307/400	1,800	Accident

Drove Southland Fire #72 Buick in all races.

A smiling trio in the winner's circle at Michigan International Speedway after Rusty won the 1994 Miller Genuine Draft 400. (left to right) Edsel B. Ford II, Rusty and Roger Penske.

1984

Date	Track/Event	St	Fn	Laps	Money	Status
2/19	Daytona/Daytona 500	27	30	95/200	$10,025	Accident
2/26	Richmond/Miller 400	5	16	396/400	4,025	Running
3/4	Rockingham/Hodgdon 500	17	26	333/492	3,590	Accident
3/18	Atlanta/Coca-Cola 500	18	19	312/328	5,040	Water Pump
4/1	Bristol/Valleydale 500	11	12	495/500	4,560	Running
4/8	N. Wilkes./N'west Bank 400	21	28	167/400	1,860	Cylinder
4/15	Darlington/TranSouth 500	24	30	175/367	3,405	Accident
4/29	Martinsville/Sovran Bank 500	14	15	491/500	4,675	Running
5/6	Talladega/Winston 500	31	31	107/188	4,580	Steering
5/12	Nashville/Coors 420	10	6	420/420	6,335	Running
5/20	Dover/Budweiser 500	14	11	495/500	6,085	Running
5/27	Charlotte/World 600	12	15	390/400	8,740	Running
6/3	Riverside/Budweiser 400	28	20	89/95	4,670	Running
6/10	Pocono/Van Scoy 500	15	17	197/200	6,530	Running
6/17	Michigan/Miller 400	11	14	199/200	7,965	Running
7/4	Daytona/Pepsi Firecracker 400	14	20	155/160	6,015	Running
7/14	Nashville/Pepsi 420	6	18	411/420	3,155	Running
7/22	Pocono/Like Cola 500	12	6	200/200	10,625	Running
7/29	Talladega/Talladega 500	10	12	188/188	8,035	Running
8/12	Michigan/Champion 400	8	35	93/200	2,715	Engine
8/25	Bristol/Busch 500	18	20	436/500	3,020	Running
9/2	Darlington/Southern 500	18	4	365/367	14,405	Running
9/9	Richmond/Wrangler 400	6	11	397/400	4,580	Running
9/16	Dover/Delaware 500	14	30	273/500	3,170	Accident
9/23	Martinsville/Goody's 500	8	13	486/500	5,015	Running
10/7	Charlotte/Miller 500	14	14	330/334	8,175	Running
10/14	N. Wilkes./Holly Farms 400	10	5	400/400	7,510	Running
10/21	Rockingham/H'don American 500	14	26	348/492	4,095	Steering
11/11	Atlanta/*Atlanta Journal* 500	16	15	320/328	6,640	Running
11/18	Riverside/Winston Western 500	26	26	105/119	3,375	Running

Drove Gatorade/Cliff Stewart Pontiac in all events; 1984 NASCAR Rookie of the Year; Finished 14th in points (3,316), 1,192 behind Winston Cup Champion Terry Labonte (4,508). In 30 starts, had two top-five finishes, four top-10 finishes and won $195,927; led races on 10 occasions; led laps in seven events; first career lap led was lap #49 during the 4/15/84 Darlington race (came in his 16th career start); drew "wild card" for the 1985 Busch Clash.

Part Four

1985

Date	Track/Event	St	Fn	Laps	Money	Status
2/17	Daytona/Daytona 500	22	8	197/200	$34,275	Running
2/21	Richmond/Miller 400	6	27	89/400	3,755	Accident
3/3	Rockingham/Carolina 500	6	9	491/492	8,675	Running
3/17	Atlanta/Coca-Cola500	10	27	196/328	5,510	Engine
4/6	Bristol/Valleydale 500	17	5	497/500	8,230	Running
4/14	TranSouth 500	20	5	365/367	11,800	Running
4/21	N. Wilkes/N'west Bank 400	7	22	386/400	3,725	Running
4/28	Martinsville/Sovran Bank 500	14	10	496/500	6,680	Running
5/5	Talladega/Winston 500	35	37	7/188	4,875	Engine
5/19	Dover/Budweiser 500	10	18	431/500	6,255	Running
5/26	Charlotte/World 600	15	8	396/400	14,695	Running
6/2	Riverside/Budweiser 400	21	24	77/95	4,880	Running
6/9	Pocono/Van Scoy 500	21	13	197/200	9,575	Engine
6/16	Michigan/Miller400	13	26	194/200	5,635	Running
7/4	Daytona/Pepsi 400	4	41	2/160	4,100	Engine
7/21	Pocono/Summer 500	13	33	112/200	4,795	Engine
7/28	Talladega/Talladega 500	23	17	183/188	7,860	Running
8/11	Michigan/Champion 400	26	7	199/200	11,395	Running
8/24	Bristol/Busch 500	21	12	487/500	5,380	Running
9/1	Darlington/Southern 500	14	38	21/367	3,880	Accident
9/8	Richmond/Wrangler 400	11	13	397/400	5,495	Running
9/15	Dover/Delaware 500	21	31	137/500	4,385	Engine
9/22	Martinsville/Goody's 500	7	25	266/500	3,935	Engine
9/29	N. Wilkes./Holly Farms 400	15	25	362/400	3,710	Running
10/6	Charlotte/Miller 500	25	30	210/334	4,540	Engine
10/20	Rockingham/Nationwise 500	14	9	489/492	8,775	Running
11/3	Atlanta/*Atlanta Journal* 500	34	21	317/328	5,560	Engine
11/17	Riverside/					
	Winston Western 500	25	36	70/119	3,500	Engine

Drove Alugard/Cliff Stewart Pontiac in all events; in 28 starts, had two top-five finishes, eight top-10 finishes and won $233,670; finished 19th in points (2,867), 1,425 points behind champion Darrell Waltrip; had 12 DNFs (10 engine failures); led first green-flag lap on lap #145 of the 4/6/85 Bristol race (in 44th career start); left Cliff Stewart operation to join Raymond Beadle's Blue Max Racing at conclusion of the 1985 season.

1986

Date	Track/Event	St	Fn	Laps	Money	Status
2/16	Daytona/Daytona 500	9	8	199/200	$37,840	Running
2/23	Richmond/Miller 400	6	10	395/400	6,530	Running
3/2	Rockingham/Carolina 500	20	12	487/492	8,165	Running
3/16	Atlanta/Motorcraft 500	7	8	327/328	12,930	Running
4/6	Bristol/Valleydale 500	14	1	500/500	34,780	Running
4/13	Darlington/TranSouth 500	13	6	364/367	12,575	Running
4/20	N. Wilkes./First Union 400	15	10	399/400	8,410	Running
4/27	Martinsville/Sovran Bank 500	5	30	56/500	7,125	Engine
5/4	Talladega/Winston 500	16	13	187/188	12,440	Running
5/18	Dover/Budweiser 500	19	26	242/500	8,400	Engine
5/25	Charlotte/Coca-Cola 600	9	10	398/400	16,750	Running
6/1	Riverside/Budweiser 400	6	4	95/95	12,775	Running
6/8	Pocono/Van Scoy 500	7	6	200/200	13,825	Running
6/15	Michigan/Miller 400	7	19	195/200	9,860	Running
7/4	Daytona/Pepsi 400	12	8	160/160	14,150	Running
7/20	Pocono/Summer 500	11	27	133/150	8,925	Engine
7/27	Talladega/Talladega 500	22	35	70/188	5,410	Engine
8/10	W'kins Glen/Bud at the Glen	4	6	90/90	14,350	Running
8/17	Michigan/Champion 400	7	6	199/200	12,525	Running
8/23	Bristol/Busch 500	12	14	484/500	7,300	Running
8/31	Darlington/Southern 500	16	23	316/367	9,710	Running
9/7	Richmond/Wrangler 400	6	19	371/400	6,960	Running
9/14	Dover/Delaware 500	8	13	491/500	9,350	Running
9/21	Martinsville/Goody's 500	8	1	500/500	40,175	Running
9/28	N. Wilkes./Holly Farms 400	5	4	400/400	10,500	Running
10/5	Charlotte/					
	Oakwood Homes 500	15	8	332/334	14,750	Running
10/19	Rockingham/Nationwise 500	7	19	453/492	9,350	Running
11/2	Atlanta/*Atlanta Journal* 500	14	13	324/328	9,585	Running
11/16	Riverside/					
	Winston Western 500	11	8	119/119	10,775	Running

Drove the Alugard/Blue Max Racing Pontiac in all events; in 29 starts, recorded two wins, four top-five finishes and 16 top-10 finishes and won $557,354; first career win came in the 4/6/86 Bristol race (72nd career start), a race in which he led three times for 174 laps; finished 6th in points (3,762), 706 points behind champion Dale Earnhardt; became 26th driver to earn over $1 million (in 96 races) in the 11/16/86 Riverside race; led first road course event during 8/10/86 Watkins Glen race (sixth road course start); led first green-flag superspeedway lap in 5/25/86 Charlotte race; recorded 1986 road course finishes of 4th, 6th and 8th.

1987

Date	Track/Event	St	Fn	Laps	Money	Status
2/15	Daytona/Daytona 500	32	41	10/200	$15,720	Piston
3/1	Rockingham/					
	Goodwrench 500	23	6	491/492	14,160	Running
3/8	Richmond/Miller 400	12	3	400/400	18,225	Running
3/15	Atlanta/Motorcraft 500	7	3	328/328	25,950	Running
3/29	Darlington/TranSouth 500	6	20	322/367	10,075	Running
4/5	N. Wilkes./First Union 400	9	9	398/400	8,685	Running
4/12	Bristol/Valleydale 500	2	16	479/500	8,710	Running
4/26	Martinsville/Sovran Bank 500	5	2	500/500	27,325	Running
5/3	Talladega/Winston 500	14	6	178/178	21,325	Running
5/24	Charlotte/Coca-Cola 600	23	10	396/400	28,375	Running
5/31	Dover/Budweiser 500	19	17	481/500	10,150	Running
6/21	Riverside/Budweiser 400	7	41	5/95	8,875	Engine
6/28	Michigan/Miller 400	1	5	200/200	25,150	Running
7/4	Daytona/Pepsi 400	6	8	160/160	15,760	Running
7/19	Pocono/Summer 500	14	14	197/200	12,765	Running
7/26	Talladega/Talladega 500	9	8	188/188	14,645	Running
8/9	W'kins Glen/Bud at the Glen	2	1	90/90	52,925	Running
8/16	Michigan/Champion 400	20	4	200/200	20,650	Running
8/22	Bristol/Busch 500	8	2	500/500	26,300	Running
9/6	Darlington/Southern 500	16	2	202/202	33,695	Running
9/13	Richmond/Wrangler 400	9	17	373/400	8,155	Accident
9/20	Dover/Delaware 500	20	12	495/500	10,900	Running
9/27	Martinsville/Goody's 500	12	28	162/500	8,200	Engine
10/4	N. Wilkes./Holly Farms 400	20	10	397/400	9,975	Running
10/11	Charlotte/					
	Oakwood Homes 500	19	22	223/334	12,065	Engine
10/25	Rockingham/Nationwise 500	17	12	489/492	11,785	Running
11/8	Riverside/					
	Winston Western 500	3	1	119/119	47,725	Running
11/22	Atlanta/*Atlanta Journal* 500	16	12	326/328	10,965	Running

Drove Kodiak/Blue Max Pontiac in all events; in 29 starts, recorded two wins, nine top-five finishes and 16 top-10 finishes and $690,652 in winnings; first career pole (and superspeedway pole) came in the 8/9/87 Michigan race (110th career race/80th on superspeedways); finished 5th in points (3,818), 878 points behind champion Dale Earnhardt; won two of three 1987 road course events.

1988

Date	Track/Event	St	Fn	Laps	Money	Status
2/14	Daytona/Daytona 500	5	7	200/200	$59,990	Running
2/21	Richmond/Pontiac 400	4	7	400/400	11,790	Running
3/6	Rockingham/Goodwrench 500	6	14	489/492	12,520	Running
3/20	Atlanta/Motorcraft 500	4	2	328/328	37,875	Running
3/27	Darlington/TranSouth 500	5	25	265/367	11,585	Engine
4/10	Bristol/Valleydale500	14	4	499/500	14,370	Running
4/17	N. Wilkes./First Union 400	3	4	400/400	14,650	Running
4/24	Martinsville/Pannill 500	2	16	488/500	12,350	Running
5/1	Talladega/Winston 500	15	10	188/188	19,300	Running
5/29	Charlotte/Coca-Cola 600	11	2	400/400	56,425	Running
6/5	Dover/Budweiser 500	11	3	500/500	26,350	Running
6/12	Riverside/Budweiser 400	2	1	95/95	49,100	Running
6/19	Pocono/Miller 500	17	3	200/200	26,500	Running
6/26	Michigan/Miller 400	5	1	200/200	64,100	Running
7/2	Daytona/Pepsi 400	19	12	159/160	13,940	Running
7/31	Talladega/Talladega 500	22	5	188/188	23,215	Running
8/14	W'kins Glen/Bud at the Glen	2	2	90/90	49,620	Running
8/21	Michigan/Champion 400	7	2	200/200	37,200	Running
8/27	Bristol/Busch 500	17	9	493/500	10,800	Running
9/4	Darlington/Southern 500	5	2	367/367	38,850	Running
9/11	Richmond/Miller 400	21	35	18/400	9,650	Accident
9/18	Dover/Delaware 500	5	3	500/500	26,200	Running
9/25	Martinsville/Goody's 500	1	3	500/500	25,825	Running
10/9	Charlotte/					
	Oakwood Homes 500	3	1	334/334	84,300	Running
10/16	N. Wilkes./Holly Farms 400	12	1	400/400	47,000	Running
10/23	Rockingham/AC Delco 500	3	1	492/492	52,150	Running
11/6	Phoenix/Checker 500	2	5	312/312	20,400	Running
11/20	Atlanta/*Atlanta Journal* 500	1	1	328/328	87,575	Running

Drove Kodiak/Blue Max Pontiac in all races; finished 2nd in points (4,464), 24 points behind champion Bill Elliott (4,488). In 29 races, recorded six wins, 19 top-five finishes, 23 top-10 finishes, two poles and $1,411,567 in winnings...eclipsed $2 million mark in 6/5/88 Dover event (became 18th driver to do so)...taking 40 races since the $1 million mark; became 14th driver to earn more than $3 million by winning the 11/20 Atlanta race (took 18 races to do so); entered the prestigious Unocal Darlington Record Club after qualifying his Pontiac at a speed of 159.761 mph; was the last driver to win a NASCAR event on the Riverside road course.

Part Four

1989

Date	Track/Event	St	Fn	Laps	Money	Status
2/19	Daytona/Daytona 500	35	18	197/200	$24,790	Running
3/5	Rockingham/					
	Goodwrench 500	1	1	492/492	72,100	Running
3/19	Atlanta/Motorcraft 500	3	31	217/328	23,110	Engine
3/26	Richmond/Pontiac 400	2	1	400/400	63,025	Running
4/2	Darlington/TranSouth 500	5	8	366/367	15,120	Running
4/9	Bristol/Valleydale 500	8	1	500/500	48,750	Running
4/16	N. Wilkes./First Union 400	1	9	399/400	16,850	Running
4/23	Martinsville/Pannill 500	9	31	272/500	10,510	Engine
5/7	Talladega/Winston 500	26	10	188/188	21,225	Running
5/28	Charlotte/Coca-Cola 600	6	31	306/400	13,950	Engine
6/4	Dover/Budweiser 500	3	5	500/500	20,975	Running
6/11	Sears Point/Banquet 300	1	2	74/74	39,225	Running
6/18	Pocono/Miller 500	1	22	194/200	16,825	Running
6/25	Michigan/Miller 400	9	2	200/200	53,025	Running
7/1	Daytona/Pepsi 400	23	17	159/160	13,580	Running
7/23	Pocono/AC 500	6	2	200/200	46,875	Running
7/30	Talladega/Diehard 500	14	37	26/188	12,225	Accident
8/13	W'kins Glen/Bud at the Glen	13	1	90/90	56,400	Running
8/20	Michigan/Champion 400	2	1	200/200	67,900	Running
8/26	Bristol/Busch 500	10	6	499/500	12,125	Running
9/3	Darlington/					
	Heinz Southern 500	5	4	367/367	24,330	Running
9/10	Richmond/Miller 400	6	1	400/400	55,650	Running
9/17	Dover/Peak 500	4	7	497/500	16,475	Running
9/24	Martinsville/Goody's 500	20	4	500/500	18,875	Running
10/8	Charlotte/All Pro 500	6	8	333/334	23,900	Running
10/15	N. Wilkes./Holly Farms 400	2	7	400/400	11,880	Running
10/22	Rockingham/AC Delco 500	21	2	492/492	33,675	Running
11/5	Phoenix/Autoworks 500	9	16	311/312	14,745	Running
11/19	Atlanta/*Atlanta Journal* 500	4	15	325/328	12,875	Running

Drove Kodiak/Blue Max Racing Pontiac in all events; 1989 NASCAR Winston Cup Champion; finished the season with 4,176 points, 12 points ahead of runner-up Dale Earnhardt (4,164); in 29 races, posted six wins, 13 top-five finishes, 20 top-10 finishes and $2,237,950 in winnings ($1,120,090 in season race earnings and $1,117,860 in post-season bonuses). Personal record for single season winnings... four pole positions and two outside poles. Became the 9th driver to earn $4 million in winning the 8/20/89 Michigan race (took 19 races since reaching the $3 million mark); became the 8th driver to win $5 million by winning the 1989 championship during the season-ending Atlanta race on 11/19/89 (took 10 races since reaching the $4 million mark).

1990

Date	Track/Event	St	Fn	Laps	Money	Status
2/18	Daytona/Daytona 500	38	7	200/200	$59,682	Running
2/25	Richmond/Pontiac 400	18	6	400/400	15,400	Running
3/4	Rockingham/					
	Goodwrench 500	7	5	490/492	21,625	Running
3/18	Atlanta/Motorcraft 500	2	24	316/328	14,930	Engine
4/1	Darlington/TranSouth 500	11	18	359/367	14,900	Running
4/8	Bristol/Valleydale 500	23	28	220/500	12,375	Accident
4/22	N. Wilkes./First Union 400	22	7	400/400	12,825	Running
4/29	Martinsville/Hanes 500	17	2	500/500	36,800	Running
5/6	Talladega/Winston 500	22	20	183/188	17,575	Running
5/27	Charlotte/Coca-Cola 600	9	1	400/400	151,000	Running
6/3	Dover/Budweiser 500	5	10	500/500	19,825	Running
6/10	Sears Point/Banquet 300	11	1	75/75	69,100	Running
6/17	Pocono/Miller 500	8	2	200/200	37,307	Running
6/24	Michigan/Miller 400	3	1	200/200	18,400	Running
7/7	Daytona/Pepsi 400	25	14	158/160	17,020	Running
7/22	Pocono/AC Spark Plug 500	8	3	200/200	30,000	Running
7/29	Talladega/DieHard 500	26	32	149/188	15,465	Engine
8/12	Watkins Glen/Bud at the Glen	4	34	46/90	15,590	Engine
8/19	Michigan/Champion 400	6	3	200/200	33,900	Running
8/25	Bristol/Busch 500	4	2	500/500	32,850	Running
9/2	Darlington/					
	Heinz Southern 500	4	40	14/367	14,400	Engine
9/9	Richmond/Miller 400	11	5	400/400	19,525	Running
9/16	Dover/Peak 500	9	7	499/500	18,175	Running
9/23	Martinsville/Goody's 500	2	15	493/500	12,825	Running
9/30	N. Wilkes./Holly Farms 400	16	8	400/400	19,525	Running
10/7	Charlotte/Mello Yello 500	12	38	133/334	11,995	Engine
10/21	Rockingham/AC Delco 500	19	32	421/492	14,075	Engine
11/4	Phoenix/Checker 500	1	38	77/312	15,975	Engine
11/18	Atlanta/*Atlanta Journal* 500	1	9	327/328	20,700	Running

Drove Miller Genuine Draft/Blue Max Racing Pontiac in all events, finished sixth in NASCAR Winston Cup points with 3,676 points. Recorded two wins, nine top five finishes, 16 top-10 finishes and two pole positions while earning $954,129.

1991

Date	Track/Event	St	Fn	Laps	Money	Status
2/17	Daytona/Daytona 500	8	27	188/200	$26,425	Accident
2/24	Richmond/Pontiac 400	20	4	400/400	13,050	Running
3/3	Rockingham/					
	Goodwrench 500	10	28	467/492	15,500	Engine
3/17	Atlanta/Motorcraft 500	3	10	327/328	6,700	Running
4/7	Darlington/TranSouth 500	21	5	365/367	10,260	Running
4/14	Bristol/Valleydale 500	1	1	500/500	51,300	Running
4/21	N. Wilkes./First Union 400	5	32	192/400	2,925	Accident
4/28	Martinsville/Hanes 500	5	21	458/500	3,750	Trans.
5/5	Talladega/Winston 500	7	28	146/188	5,645	Running
5/26	Charlotte/Coca-Cola 600	9	22	353/400	7,000	Engine
6/2	Dover/Budweiser 500	2	9	498/500	9,950	Running
6/9	Sears Point/Banquet 300	4	3	74/74	34,975	Running
6/16	Pocono/Champion 500	9	31	115/200	4,775	Engine
6/23	Michigan/MGD 400	23	17	198/200	6,925	Running
7/6	Daytona/Pepsi 400	28	12	160/160	9,600	Running
7/21	Pocono/MGD 500	10	1	200/200	34,100	Running
7/28	Talladega/DieHard 500	8	6	188/188	16,250	Running
8/11	W'kinsGlen/Bud at the Glen	21	4	90/90	16,680	Running
8/18	Michigan/Champion 400	9	3	200/200	23,600	Running
8/24	Bristol/Bud 500	2	32	88/500	4,425	Accident
9/1	Darlington/Southern 500	13	32	214/367	5,045	Engine
9/7	Richmond/MGD 400	1	3	400/400	21,700	Running
9/15	Dover/Peak 500	7	25	322/500	5,025	Accident
9/22	Martinsville/Goody's 500	7	7	500/500	11,500	Running
9/29	N. Wilkes./Holly Farms 400	7	6	400/400	8,950	Running
10/6	Charlotte/Mellow Yellow 500	8	7	296/334	4,775	Running
10/20	Rockingham/AC Delco 500	9	11	489/492	9,000	Running
11/3	Phoenix/Pyroil 500	10	5	312/312	16,475	Running
11/17	Atlanta/Hardee's 500	24	34	197/328	4,025	Accident

First year as driver/co-owner of Miller Genuine Draft Team Penske Pontiac Racing Team; finished 10th in NASCAR Winston Cup points with 3,582 points. Recorded two wins, nine top-five finishes, 14 top-10 finishes and two pole positions while earning $502,073.

1992

Date	Track/Event	St	Fn	Laps	Money	Status
2/16	Daytona/Daytona 500	17	31	150/200	$30,455	Running
3/1	Rockingham/					
	Goodwrench 500	5	26	442/492	13,100	O'heat.
3/8	Richmond/Pontiac 400	12	17	396/400	12,425	Running
3/15	Atlanta/Motorcraft 500	12	15	327/328	14,980	Running
3/29	Darlington/TranSouth 500	19	11	364/367	14,665	Running
4/5	Bristol/Food City 500	3	9	494/500	15,280	Running
4/12	N. Wilkes./First Union 400	5	2	400/400	29,140	Running
4/26	Martinsville/Hanes 500	7	31	178/500	11,000	Engine
5/3	Talladega/Winston 500	18	11	188/188	18,530	Running
5/24	Charlotte/Coca-Cola 600	7	18	386/400	18,050	Engine
5/31	Dover/Budweiser 500	14	3	499/500	25,795	Running
6/7	Sears Point/Save Mart 300	3	7	74/74	18,110	Running
6/14	Pocono/Champion 500	10	24	185/200	13,250	Running
6/21	Michigan/MGD 400	8	7	69/200	13,465	Camshaft
7/4	Daytona/Pepsi 400	29	9	160/160	18,325	Running
7/19	Pocono/MGD 500	19	18	199/200	13,690	Running
7/26	Talladega/Diehard 500	28	11	187/188	17,220	Running
8/9	W'kins Glen/Bud at the Glen	8	6	51/51	18,240	Running
8/16	Michigan/Champion 400	33	21	198/200	15,040	Running
8/29	Bristol/Bud 500	8	10	498/500	14,575	Running
9/6	Darlington/Southern 500	21	9	298/298	17,060	Running
9/12	Richmond/MGD 400	3	1	400/400	47,115	Running
9/20	Dover/Peak 500	3	17	483/500	13,730	Running
9/28	Martinsville/Goody's 500	8	2	500/500	39,400	Running
10/5	N. Wilkes./Holly Farms 400	2	4	399/400	18,600	Running
10/11	Charlotte/Mello Yellow 500	21	38	128/334	11,590	Carbur.
10/25	Rockingham/AC Delco 500	9	21	485/492	16,700	Running
11/1	Phoenix/Pyroil 500	1	28	295/312	26,735	Running
11/15	Atlanta/Hooters 500	15	6	328/328	20,100	Running

In his second year as combination driver/co-owner, Wallace recorded one win, five top-five finishes, 12 top-10 finishes, one pole position and earned $657,925; finished 13th in the NASCAR Winston Cup points with 3,556 points.

In the winner's circle at Bristol, Rusty and Patti are all smiles after Rusty won the 1994 Goody's 500. Note Rusty's new uniform, designed by Roger Penske.

1993

Date	Track/Event	St	Fn	Laps	Money	Status
2/14	Daytona/Daytona 500 By STP	34	32	168/200	$38,600	Crash
2/28	Rockingham/					
	Goodwrench 500	10	1	492/492	42,735	Running
3/7	Richmond/					
	Pontiac Excitement 400	13	2	400/400	31,550	Running
3/20	Atlanta/Motorcraft 500	1	3	328/328	41,550	Running
3/28	Darlington/TranSouth 500	3	5	366/367	20,400	Running
4/4	Bristol/Food City 500	1	1	500/500	107,610	Running
4/18	N. Wilkes./First Union 400	9	1	400/400	43,535	Running
4/25	Martinsville/Hanes 500	5	1	500/500	45,175	Running
5/2	Talladega/Winston 500	24	6	188/188	28,490	Flying
5/16	Sears Point/Save Mart 300	6	38	64/74	15,615	Trans.
5/30	Charlotte/Coca-Cola 600	8	29	353/400	14,880	Handling
6/6	Dover/Budweiser 500	4	21	425/500	17,450	Crash
6/13	Pocono/Champion 500	10	39	4/200	14,285	Engine
6/20	Michigan/MGD 400	15	5	200/200	26,160	Running
7/3	Daytona/Pepsi 400	17	18	160/160	16,870	Running
7/11	Loudon/Slick 50 300	33	1	300/300	77,500	Running
7/18	Pocono/MGD 500	18	2	200/200	35,145	Running
7/25	Talladega/Diehard 500	32	17	188/188	17,900	Running
8/8	W'kins Glen/Bud at the Glen	6	19	90/90	16,105	Running
8/15	Michigan/Champion 400	10	6	200/200	24,115	Running
8/28	Bristol/Bud 500	2	2	500/500	31,875	Running
9/5	Darlington/					
	Mt. Dew South. 500	11	3	351/351	27,495	Running
9/11	Richmond/MGD 400	3	1	400/400	49,415	Running
9/19	Dover/SplitFire 500	1	1	500/500	77,645	Running
9/26	Martinsville/Goody's 500	4	2	500/500	31,875	Running
10/3	N.Wilkes./Tyson 400	11	1	400/400	46,260	Running
10/10	Charlotte/Mello Yellow 500	21	4	334/334	42,950	Running
10/24	Rockingham/AC Delco 500	18	1	492/492	52,850	Running
10/31	Phoenix/Slick 50 500	6	19	310/312	15,495	Running
11/14	Atlanta/Hooters 500	20	1	328/328	93,100	Running

Third season behind the wheel of the Miller Genuine Draft Team Penske Pontiac; won 10 races for his all-time season high; also recorded 19 top-fives and 21 top-10s along with 3 pole positions; after two wild crashes (uninjured in crash at Daytona on 2/14; received slight concussion and broken left wrist in 5/2 crash at Talladega) team mounted serious challenge for the points title...finished 2nd in points, 80 points behind Dale Earnhardt. Penkse Team won the annual Unocal Pit Crew Championship at Rockingham, establishing a new world's record (22.454 seconds); led most laps during the season (2,860 of 10,004=28.6%).

To us, you'll always be #1.

Thank you Rusty, for giving us so many great rides.